Canadianity

HarperCollins*Publishers*Ltd

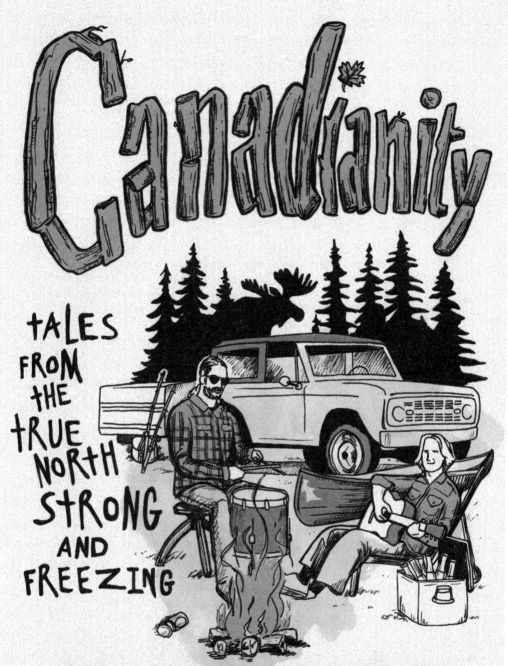

Canadianity

tALES FROM tHE tRUE NORtH STRONG AND FREEZING

JEREMY TAGGART AND JONATHAN TORRENS

Canadianity
Copyright © 2017 by Taggart & Torrens Inc.
All rights reserved.

· Published by HarperCollins Publishers Ltd

First edition

Tips by *Canadianity* Bahd Ambassadors (used with permission):
PEI: Patrick Ledwell; **Cape Breton:** Bette MacDonald; **Montreal:** Jared Keeso; **Winnipeg:** Jay Onrait, Brittney Thomas-Ljungberg; **Regina:** Andrea Dion; **Saskatoon:** Neil Barron and Dave Murray/*Maple Syrup Shots*; Jay Onrait; **Edmonton:** Tom Gazzola, Chris Wescott and Ryan Frankson; **Alberta:** Jay Onrait, Reid Wilkins; **British Columbia:** Rikki F.; **Newfoundland and Labrador:** Andrew O'Brien and Cat Allan/Fortunate Ones

Stories by *Canadianity* contributors (used with permission):
Kevin Perry (tire game); Warren Mulvey (bottle game); Philip Kurut (throwing rocks); Graham Metzger (price check); and Dead "Deaner" Briggs (arrow game)

Line drawings by Jud Haynes

HarperCollins books may be purchased for educational, business, or sales promotional use through our Special Markets Department.

HarperCollins Publishers Ltd
2 Bloor Street East, 20th Floor
Toronto, Ontario, Canada
M4W 1A8

www.harpercollins.ca

Library and Archives Canada Cataloguing in Publication information is available upon request.

ISBN 978-1-44344-929-8

Printed and bound in the United States of America
LSC/C 10 9 8 7 6 5 4 3 2

For Beryl & Ronnie. —Taggart

For Pat & Susan. Thanks for taking a whack at it. —Torrens

Contents

A Warm Welcome

Hey, bahd! Congratulations on buying this book! Don't let anyone tell you that you didn't accomplish something today.

Unless maybe your aunt who doesn't know you that well gave it to you for your birthday. Or you just got transferred to a job in the Great White North and a colleague gave it to you as a joke "Canadian primer." Or you found an old Indigo gift card when you were cleaning out the Kia and grabbed this off the clearance table beside the cash before the card expired.

No matter how this glorious tome ended up in your hands, welcome! We're glad you're here.

What you're about to read/skim in the bathroom/use as kindling is a celebration of the clich-ehs we Canadians sometimes roll our collective eyes at. We call them clich-ehs. (**Torrens:** Okay, I do. Taggart doesn't dig wordplay as much as me.)

Really, though. Doesn't it seem like people are prouder than ever to call Canada home? Especially the more that other parts of the world are in turmoil. We think this particular chest-puffing period started around 2010, during the Vancouver Olympics. Media from around the world reported that "Canada is cool," as though this was somehow breaking news. We always knew it. All right, we *suspected* it, even if it wasn't something we would dare say out loud. That would be too braggy. If there's one thing we Canadians are not, it's that.

Canada's current cool chapter has continued ever since. Tatiana Maslany won an Emmy for her astonishing work on *Orphan Black*. Astronaut Chris Hadfield's singing-from-space video went viral globally. Canada Goose has a flagship store in Manhattan. Even our prime minister (another JT) upped the ante, with photo spreads of him and his wife spooning, gazing, even necking appearing in fashion magazines. Because it's 2016. Or it was then. On the night Donald Trump became president-elect, the Canadian Immigration and Citizenship ministry's website crashed because Americans were curious about escaping to a better life here in the Great White North.

We've certainly enjoyed this outbreak of pride on our *Taggart & Torrens* podcast, when we made up a word—"Canadianity"—to describe what it means to have Canada as your home and native land. *Canadianity.* It sounds vaguely religious, and at first we were using it borderline facetiously.

It wasn't until we asked our listeners to define it that we realized we were really on to something. Some definitions were macro, as you might expect. Being kind. Enjoying wilderness. Sewing flags on our backpacks.

But it was the ones that were so hyper-specific that caught our attention.

"Your beer-league goalie bursts into the dressing room three minutes before you take the ice."

"Paying for the Timmies for the guy behind you in drive-thru."

"Listening to the Hip while opening the cottage on May 2-4."

And so this new religion was born: Canadianity. Also known as Bahddism. Everywhere we go we meet more and more practising Bahddists. Turns out *TnT* was filling a hole we didn't even know existed. Filling it with nostalgia and cultural references that had long ago been buried in snow. Not, like, Snow the rapper. Actual snow. Canadian snow.

Or was it frozen tears from a time not so long ago when nobody chose Albert? 'Member that commercial for Canadian Tire?

So, back to the clich-ehs. Knowing that we're now using them to define Canadianity with pride, let's begin with the biggest one of all.

Canadians are nice.

So what? We are.

We apologize too much. Also true.

But we're not "sorry aboot that," because it's in our DNA, and frankly, of all the reputations we could have, "nice" is a pretty nice one. It's better than cheap, aggressive or not fresh.

By the way, the only time you ever really hear someone say "aboot" is when an American is trying to mock us. That's okay too.

We're far more offended by their use of the phrase "ice hockey," as if there's any other kind. If you ever want to raise the ire of an American, find a way to slip the term "grass baseball" into a conversation. We're more likely to say "aboat" than "aboot" anyway. So there.

What are some of the other clich-ehs?

That we love maple syrup. Hardly a diss, but okay. Who could blame us? It's *delicious*, as we were reminded in our original *TnT* game 50/50 Shots, where you have to pound a shot of maple syrup if you give the wrong answer to a trivia question. Warning: Do not play this game with Aunt Jemima. Or with an actual Mountie, as we did at our live show in Regina. It results in a Canadianity OD and can leave you feeling slightly nauseated.

Speaking of Mounties, how about the clich-eh that members of the RCMP are squeaky-clean, earnest folks—"Dudley Do-Right meets *Due South*" types? True. But aren't those good qualities for the ones protecting us?

We have free health care. Again, true. Less of a clich-eh and more of an interesting tidbit straight out of a "So You Want to Converse with a Canadian" handbook.

Although realistically, if you go to the emergency room with a splinter, you might be waiting a long time while all the people with massive head wounds from errant skate blades get treated.

Here's another generalization: Canadian female singers have only one name. Céline. Alanis. Shania. Tagaq. Drake. So? They've sold squadrillions of records and are household names all over the world!

Oh yeah. That we're hosers, as portrayed by Bob and Doug McKenzie. I mean, that one's not exactly wrong either. But we've been called worse.

That's pretty much it. In a nutshell, those are the preconceived notions the rest of the world has "aboat" us. Pretty harmless overall.

Why do we care? Really, why does it matter what others think about us?

What it comes down to is that it would be rude *not* to care, and we Canadians are extremely polite.

Like most clich-ehs, these are born out of at least a kernel of truth. So we can either get our backs up and be defensive about them or just allow that they're at least partly true and get in on the joke. The latter makes so much more sense, especially because another thing we are for sure is funny.

Like Mike Myers, Jim Carrey, Catherine O'Hara, Martin Short, Eugene Levy, Samantha Bee, Rick Mercer, John Candy funny. Pretty impressive pedigree. It's because our humour has a British influence, but our proximity to America determines a lot of our pop culture. These two distinct flavours combined with our own homegrown self-deprecating quality create a Neapolitan of comedic sensibilities. Cheeky, witty, silly.

Our pop-culture landscape is as diverse as our geography. Canada is responsible for Blue Rodeo and Bublé, for Pamela Anderson and Steve Nash, for Rush and the Weeknd. We export hockey players and import baseball players. We watch American reality shows but take great pride in confessing to how sheepish we are about it before making our own softer, gentler versions, like *Survivor: Sudbury*. We can relate to *Letterkenny Problems*, and we all know at least a few *Trailer Park Boys*.

The truth is it's hard to make sweeping generalizations about Canada because the culture of this country is as diverse as the landscape itself. Vast arctic tundra and endless prairie wheat fields, cookie-cutter cliffs and mighty mountains, lakes and rivers, ponds and streams. Space. Fresh air. Cleanliness. We see plenty of that when we take *Taggart & Torrens* on tour across this great land. It's shocking how many times you can say "hoarfrost" on the drive across Saskatchewan.

Some of us do live in igloos, but most of us don't. Most of us do live within a hundred miles of the US border. We get irritated when Americans can't name all the provinces, though most of us can't name all of the states.

We invented basketball and butter tarts, insulin and the telephone, the jolly jumper and the Wonderbra (two separate things it turns out).

Here's a trivia question for you. The Robertson screwdriver (another Canadian invention) was named after:

a. Lloyd Robertson

b. Robertson Davies

c. Ed Robertson of Barenaked Ladies, whose real first name is Lloyd

None of the above.

Here's some more trivia for you. Trivial Pursuit was invented by Canadians. As was *Hockey Night in Canada. Speakers' Corner. The Royal Canadian Air Farce.*

Stompin' Tom. Rita MacNeil.

Is your heart swelling with pride? *No?* Are you sure you're even Canadian?

To be sure one way or the other, take our very short *TnT* Canadianity quiz. If you answer yes to most of these questions, you're as Canuck as Steve Podborski.

1. Do you know who Steve Podborski is?
2. Have you ever bought something with Club Z points?
3. Do you have an Optimum card/Aeroplan miles/Canadian Tire money?
4. Can you say, "The one with McCain punch" with a straight face?
5. Were you taught to "play safe"?
6. Is Maple Leaf your national symbol *and* your luncheon meat?

7. Do you know who Hal and Joanne are?

8. Did you ever get Roots boots for Christmas?

9. Have you ever celebrated Bad Days?

10. Did you roadtrip to Alberta or Quebec for your eighteenth birthday?

11. Does "Snowbird" refer to a plane, people who go south in the winter *and* an Anne Murray song?

12. Have you ever spent a Friday night at the *Electric Circus* studio?

How did you do? Do you feel like you've just completed the *20-Minute Workout* (that's worth a Google)? If you answered yes to the majority of these questions, you're as Canadian as a GST refund cheque.

If you didn't, get reading, bahd! You have work to do. And so do we . . .

Over the next several hundred pages, we'll fly the flag with pride and shine a light on some of the people, places and faces that make this country so great from coast to coast to coast.

Please note: this is not the definitive list. This is OUR *Taggart & Torrens* list, cobbled together from our trans-Canada adventures and misadventures. So don't bother pointing out that we forgot the Gaétan Boucher "skating on butter" ad. 'Cuz we may well have.

Along the way, we'll also share some Tales from the Road about how this country has shaped us into the soon-to-hopefully-receive-honorary-doctorates-from-some-low-end-university men we are today. Jeremy's two decades touring the country with Our Lady Peace have resulted in some doozies. Jonathan's travels with *Street Cents*, *Jonovision* and *Trailer Park Boys* have yielded some solid yarns too, although maybe overall a little less rock 'n' roll in tone.

We'll even throw in our suggestions—and some of yours—for the best places to [insert aggressive action verb] food across the country.

So grab a donair and a frosty soldier, put on your best Beaver Canoe rugby shirt with matching Cooperalls, and settle in for a journey through Canadianity.

Let's start at the start. What the hell even is *Taggart & Torrens*?

The Poddy and the Page Turn

Torrens

The shelf life of a "celebrity" in Canada is relatively short. Just ask the cast of any high-profile original CTV drama from the 2000s. Or the members of b4-4. Or Alligator Al from *Mr. Dressup*. However, there is one exception to this rule: if you make it big in the States.

Or if you're Rick Mercer.

Or if you're a hockey analyst. Or a star in Quebec. Or Anne Murray. Or named Gord.

Okay, so there are a few exceptions, but generally we Canadians tend to think that as soon as someone achieves any amount of success on screen, it's someone else's turn. One and done. Hard to build a star system this way, but I guess it's the Canadian Way in that more people get a shot.

It's not lost on me just how lucky I am to have worked for twenty-five years-plus in the business here. Pretty sure I've managed to stick around for two reasons:

1. I've never been the star of my own big prime-time show. Instead, I'm usually second to seventh banana on a high-profile show, or on a kids show, which has allowed me to fly under the radar. Hard to get overexposed on a Saturday morning consumer-affairs show for kids.

2. The 180. Doing *Trailer Park Boys* after *Jonovision* was such a change-up, so out of left field, that it allowed people to see me in a whole different way. Same as playing buttoned-up Robert Cheeley on *Mr. D* after sporting track suits and Ardene bling as J-Roc on *Trailer Park Boys*.

The last thing you can afford to be in a market this size is typecast. It's the Dan Hill factor. After "Sometimes When We Touch," most people saw him as a saccharine balladeer instead of the hardcore folkie he was before that.

Here's the other harsh reality: I couldn't be J-Roc for a living. Creatively or financially. Even if I could combine shooting the series in the summer and touring as a fake rapper in the winter, that might last a few years. Then what?

So, like a junkie, I'm always looking for my next buzz. How can I change it up?

Shooting scripted shows is fun, especially ones like *TPB* and *Mr. D*, where we're allowed to riff in and out of the script. Improv keeps you on your toes and keeps it fresh. But there's a lull between shooting and when the show is released—sometimes up to six months.

So I was looking to do something with a more immediate turnaround. Especially in this day and age, where feedback is instantaneous and you can incorporate it into your show as it evolves.

Something lo-fi, where there was maybe less money, lower stakes and fewer resources involved, but ultimately more creative control. In other words, something that, for better or for worse, was exactly what I meant.

Since *Trailer Park Boys* has been on Netflix, we've been spoiled. There isn't a network executive weighing in with copious script notes like "I don't think that character should be called Marsha because I went to school with a Marsha and she was nothing like that." It's a dream scenario and I'd gotten kinda used to doing/saying/writing what I wanted.

Enter Jeremy Taggart. We'd met over the years. We were fringe friends—definitely aware of each other but not close. I'd heard him on *The Jay & Dan Podcast*, hosted by beloved TSN personalities Jay Onrait and Dan O'Toole, and thought he was funny. His story-telling style and experiences were so different from mine. Plus, I think we all secretly wonder what it would be like to be a rock star, and having a friend you can drill with questions about it is right up my alley.

"What if you got a blister on your thumb before a big show? Would you cancel?"

"What if you have to pee during a set?"

"Have you ever trashed a hotel room?"

The timing couldn't have been better. He was ready for a page turn after leaving Our Lady Peace.

Here's what a lot of people don't know: bands like OLP were instrumental to the success of *Trailer Park Boys* early on. The show had trouble getting traction in its first season or two. It looked and sounded different from anything else that came before it. The TV landscape wasn't quite ready for "*Cops* from a criminal's point of view."

Fortunately, bands started watching the DVDs of the show on their tour buses. They'd pass them back and forth, share them with friends. Soon, pro sports teams were watching too.

Still, it's safe to say it wasn't exactly a ratings juggernaut when Jeremy suggested that Ricky, Julian and Bubbles go on tour with Our Lady Peace as the opening act. I'm sure the other members of his band scratched their heads at this notion. What on earth would they do? They weren't a band.

For whatever reason, the idea went ahead, and Taggs often talks about witnessing Trailer Park fever strike as they made their way across the country. Band and boys. Slowly, surely, audiences were starting to not only buy in but really dig it.

"Knock knock," Ricky would say to an arena full of people.

"Who's there?" they'd reply.

"Go f*ck yourself!"

Cheers would go up throughout the venue. People suddenly couldn't get enough of the Sunnyvale crew.

Other bands like Rush and the Hip helped too, and soon *Trailer Park Boys* was well on its way. So thanks, Taggs, for helping me play J-Roc for fifteen years to the point where people were like "Why is that doughy dad wearing a do-rag?"

The Explosion of TnT

Taggart

I've known Jonathan since around 2004. Mike Smith of *Trailer Park Boys* always appreciated my skill for comparing random people with noted celebrities, the more obscure, the better the chuckle. Mike told me I had to experience Jonathan's same gift.

I finally met Jono at a charity golf tournament in Toronto. We were paired together and we had a spectacular back-and-forth on the first tee. I told him I hoped he played as well as his looka-like, Jack Wagner, and he swiped back by calling me a Father of Confederation, what with my long hair all tied up and falling about. A solid thump by Torrens, earning my respect forever thereafter.

We kept in touch and always kept in mind that we'd like to work together at some point. It wasn't until I started becoming a regu-lar on *The Jay & Dan Podcast* that I realized that's what we should do. People were digging the tales about my dad and the road, and I was looking into ways of having my own pod with interesting guests. When Jonathan went on with Jay and Dan, with his ridiculous Sobeys bag story, he had a very similar reaction to mine. I gave him a ring and asked if he'd be into doing a podcast together. He agreed that it would probably be fun, so we made a demo at Newstalk 1010, a radio station in Toronto, with the help of Mike Bendixen, the station's program director and a great bahd. We had such a great time doing the demo that we just started making pods and firing them onto SoundCloud.

A great friend of mine, Tim Oxford, who used to edit my old podcast, *Taggart's Take*, got on board as well to put the files together and drop in fave bits in the breaks. He's been such an important part of *TnT*. When he's not too busy drumming in his band, the Arkells, he's editing our episodes together in dressing rooms, hotels or tour buses. Such a great guy from a great family that I've known since the late '90s.

The fact we were just enjoying the conversation was the fire that built and maintains *TnT* today. It's really just two bahds having a good chat. The buzz was always generated at the grassroots through word of mouth. We always said we'd be huge if we could get the podcast onto iTunes—an ongoing joke for about a year after we started—and oh boy, when we hit iTunes in January of 2015 (thanks to technical bahd Mike MacFarlane), the Canadianity hit the fan! We instantly saw our download numbers skyrocket—a couple thousand downloads an episode became fifteen thousand plus. People started binge-listening to us and the mail started pouring in from bahds all over Canada and even the world. Folks were saying they felt like they were in the room with us. They were laughing out loud on buses or while walking down the street, getting weird looks from others. They were escaping with us for an hour of their lives, just enjoying the Canadianity, right up to two million downloads!

Hitting the road was the next thing we wanted to do—to find the bahds in person, so we could get a better idea of who they are and, in a way, find out the true meaning of Canadianity.

Torrens

It's kind of full circle for Jeremy and me to be doing *Taggart & Torrens*. People often ask what we intended when we started. Not sure we really knew. Pretty sure we still don't. But we quickly bonded over John Candy, absurd characters in peculiar situations, and this beautiful country.

I'm "that guy from that show." He's "that guy from that band." Together, we're candid and curious. Cautious and adventurous. Taggart and Torrens.

On the surface, we might be different, but our core values are the same. We both started out on our professional paths at a pretty young age. We're both family men with a low tolerance for arrogance. Taggs is probably softer than he lets on, and I might be harder. We both love to tell and be told a good story.

Also, as insignificant as it may seem, *Taggart & Torrens* sounds good together. People love alliteration. We're both JTs. Our names have the same number of syllables. We had a short conversation early on about whether it should be *Taggart & Torrens* or *Torrens & Taggart*, and both agreed it should be the former.

I have a theory that it's because your ear hears "tattered and torn," so it just feels right. Also, ever notice how, with "couple friends," there's a name order that works better? "Travis 'n' Tina" flows better than "Tina 'n' Travis." Same thing with *TnT*.

Jeremy's good for me, in that he's more apt to just "feel it," whereas

I'm apt to produce it. Given my background, I really wanted us at first to at least have tent poles so we had something to hold the episodes up. A guest in segment one, a game in segment two, a story in segment three.

Turns out we didn't need that. In fact, the less we prepared, the more we just riffed and spritzed, the more bahds liked it. And so did we, actually. It was fun to freestyle without a net. The risk/reward ratio is higher because sometimes things fall flat, but when they work, they *really* work.

Podcast purists have taught me a lot. Terrestrial radio is limiting because you have to listen Wednesday at eight. Pod bahds want to download six eps and listen to them all while ice fishing on Saturday afternoon. Or on the drive to their folks' cottage at the lake. Or in their cubicle while pretending to work.

Podcasts are to radio what the internet is to TV. It gives all the control to the consumer. Once I wrapped my head around that, it was so freeing.

Almost like the TPB/Netflix experience, *TnT* doesn't have anyone at the "network" weighing in on our Top Fives, or suggesting that our workplace morning-radio sketch "Jer Bear and Colleen in the Morning" is sexist. It isn't sexist, it's a parody of a man and woman who hate each other but are forced to work together. This happens in real life and is worthy of mocking. Especially the part where he makes more than she does.

A character like sexy Spaniard Salvador, for example, would probably never make it to TV because it would fall under the banner of cultural stereotyping. It was absolutely born out of that clich-eh— just like Canadians being nice—but dialled up to a cartoonish outlandish degree.

The thing about comedy (which *TnT* is some of the time) is that it has to reflect someone's point of view. When it tries to be all things to all people, it stops being anything to anyone. That's often why network comedies don't work. Too many cooks. At *TnT* we have only two cooks.

All this to say we're drunk on our own power. That's the upside. The downside is we don't get paid. Like, at all. Creative freedom also means we're not weighed down by any stacks of money. But that's okay. We started doing the show for the right reasons and the rest will fall into place.

After all, here we are writing a book for HarperCollins, no less. *There's* a page turn no one saw coming.

When we started touring across the country, we realized that BAHDdism was bigger than both of us. It's a full-on religion. Bahds were making plans to meet up beforehand and promising to stay in touch afterwards, bringing us pictures, stickers and stories.

It was so uplifting to see the pride folks showed in this country and how the poddy had brought them together. We've heard countless stories of how bahds have found each other in the unlikeliest of places. Almost like a secret handshake, a whispered question—"Are you a bahd too?"—unlocking the code to instant friendship.

The best compliment we get is that listeners feel like they're sitting in the backseat listening to two bahds shoot the poo up front. I'm always surprised at how a character we made up and only appeared once in, say, episode 7, will stick with people. To the point where people will call out, "Do Malcolm!" at a live show and we look at each other like "Who's Malcolm?"

Maybe the biggest kick we get is from hearing from folks overseas—teaching English or hiking or foolishly chasing love—saying the poddy is like a care package from home. I dig that so much, thinking of people half a world away, eagerly anticipating this little weekly ping from across the pond as a remedy for homesickness. Tim Hortons Chicken Soup for the Wandering Canadian Soul.

See, *that's* what we should've called this book.

So there's Canadianity nailed down. One last bit of business before we hit the road across the country on this epic word journey: in true Canadianity fashion, we didn't want to place the provincial chapters in any particular order, suggesting that west was somehow best or east was least. So we started with Prince Edward Island and Ontario because we were born there and we thought it'd give you the chance to get to know us a little better. From there, we jumped around more than Tie Domi in a tilt.

Canadianity Glossary

Here are some other *TnT* terms that you might find useful.

Alan Doyle A term coined by Jeremy, used as a verb, that means to fall on the sidewalk but recover gracefully. "I Alan Doyled it right in front of the bus stop!"

Alert alert! Borrowed from Jeremy's daughter, Aneliese. "Alert alert! John is taking a cookie!" or "Alert alert! Glass Tiger tickets go on sale today!"

bahd Slang for "bud." One who is kind in the way only Canadians can be. "Thanks for lending me your Sherwood PMP stick for street hockey, bahd!"

Bahddism The religion of being a bahd. There is a Bahddist movement.

birlin' The act of log rolling. Rose to fame in the classic animated National Film Board interstitial *Log Driver's Waltz*. "I'm birlin' into the Legion because it's Friday night—buck-a-pitcher on draft!"

Bruce A jerk. "Some Bruce parked behind me and I can't get out."

butterfly laughter According to the Orange Julius website, this is the mystery ingredient in its delicious beverages.

Canadianity As discussed, too personal to define. For us, it's hundreds of bahds showing up at a live *TnT* show in Saskatoon during a snowstorm.

Canajianwaysss What Jonathan's South American character Salvador admittedly doesn't understand after his pervy advances are rebuffed.

classic Taggart's label for something instantly unforgettably funny.

crunch crunch crunch The sound of a greasy businessman freshening his breath with Tic Tacs before getting right into things with a lady.

darts Cigarettes. "I didn't know Kelsey was on the darts!"

day boiler Daytime drinking session resulting in getting drunk.

Frig off, pecker! On the *TnT* fake sitcom *Andrea N Them*, Jonathan's East Coaster character Andrea uses this as her flirty catchphrase.

ghirlst How PEI magician Mr. Magic pronounces "girls" (in Jonathan's mind, at least). "What did yas do with the eggs, ghirlst?"

Holy boats! A Taggart staple meaning "wow."

peanut brutal Torrens's way of expressing that something was awful.

right friggy How Andrea describes the feeling in her tummy when she's nervous.

right on In this case, a seemingly positive response, used to diffuse a negative situation. It's hard to combat. "I overcharged you? Right on!"

taquitos A culinary delicacy served only at Irving gas stations.

weekend bumsies When you're not officially on the darts but might hit someone up for the odd one on the sidewalk outside the bar.

whatev-salad Taggart's expression for "Who cares?"

yaz Second-person plural in the Maritimes. "Are yaz coming over for dinner?"

Yiker's Island A bastardized version of "yikes," paired with New York penitentiary Rikers Island.

Prince Edward Island: Spuds and Bahds

Bahd Bands

Haywire

Paper Lions

Cat MacLellan

Tim Chaisson

Boxcar Dan

Rose Cousins

Raccoon Bandit

Al Tuck

Kinley Dowling

Lennie Gallant

Five Notable Bahds

Boomer Gallant. CBC weatherman. Local legend. Used to call the harness races.

Brad Richards. NHLer from a fishing town. Won a coupla Cups.

Heather Moyse. Her sports resumé is undeniable: three-time Olympian, two-time gold medal winner, multisport athlete who has repped Canada on the world stage in bobsleigh, rugby and cycling. But it's her charitable work that elevates her to true bahd status: Right to Play, Special Olympics, Camp Triumph and Boys & Girls Clubs, among others.

Lorie Kane. First female golfer from PEI to be *best in the world*.

Matthew. Anne of Green Gables's uncle. Despite Anne's shenanigans and Marilla's constant nitpicking, Matthew held it down, being a constant and calm presence for that girl with the red hair.

The Fixed Link

Torrens

It makes sense to begin where it all began, with the Fathers of Confederation in the birthplace of our nation, PEI. Now, *those* bahds could put away some suds.

I was born in Charlottetown and lived in Sherwood, just outside of town, until I was about twelve. What an incredible place to call home, especially in the summer.

I remember getting to the cottage on Friday nights and realizing we'd forgotten something at home—hamburger buns, say, or one of my siblings. My mother would say, "I'm not driving all the way back to get it."

All the way back. Fifteen minutes. It didn't even occur to me at the time that the Island might be small. It was all I knew.

Every time I'm home, my senses become heightened. The mud is so red, the grass so green, the sky so blue. On the south shore, the water is so warm. On the north shore, the sand is so white. On the dunes at Greenwich near St. Peters, the coastline is seemingly endless. But you might find yourself suddenly in a turf war with aggressive seagulls who aren't used to sharing the unspoiled beach.

And yes, the people are so friendly. The fish, lobster and oysters are so fresh. Cows ice cream is so good. Might I suggest the Gooey Mooey?

It's a magical place, and if you're from there, you know this. If you visit, you can feel it. One year at the Rick Vaive Celebrity Golf Classic in Charlottetown, as a kid I watched Gretzky drain a 7-iron from 180 yards right into the cup. See? Magic.

As kids, we also frequented a place in Cavendish called Rainbow Valley that prominently featured a gift shop that was a *spaceship*. This was a routine destination for us, and nobody found it odd. On PEI, anything was possible.

In typical small-town fashion, people still give directions based on dated landmarks. "Turn left where the Esso used to be, and then it's just before Elliot's place." Some still call it Towers Mall when Towers department store hasn't been there since Trudeau (the OG Trudeau).

There was something so comforting about growing up on an island. It was like the isolation made us somehow safe from harm. We even "banned the can" in the interest of public safety. Then suddenly a fixed-link bridge was up for discussion, and Islanders worried about "Moncton crazies" coming over every weekend and burning the place to the ground. Like they had nothing better to do.

On the plus side, it turned out the fixed link would also give us Islanders a way to escape the long winter months. I'm talking "no school for five days until our road could get plowed" winter. High winds. Flat surface. Major snow. Ferries and flights cancelled.

On a side note, they used to interview tourists live on CFCY radio as they waited for the ferry. Where are you from? What did you do on the Island? Those kinds of questions. I once heard a woman from Georgia say, in her sweet southern drawl, "My husband and I had the nahcest tahm here on PE-1."

PE-1? How long were you *on* PE-1 that no one set you straight on that?

That bridge was such a crazy undertaking. They used satellite technology to place the concrete girders in the ocean, and they could land them within one millimetre of accuracy. Bananas for back then. The thing that really blew my mind as a kid is that they had accounted for a certain number of deaths in the building of the bridge. Makes sense, I suppose, that a project of that magnitude would have crazy risk, but imagine working in that environment, where people are expected to die! Yikes. "Have a great afternoon out there, Terry. No dying, eh?"

At least they came in under budget on that front.

They held a contest to name the bridge, and one Grade 5 class came up with "Span of Green Cables," which I thought was genius. That might've been my introduction to wordplay. It's a love affair that's lasted my whole life. A solid bon mot makes me feel warm and fuzzy, like a homemade cozy for my heart made out of yarn spun from the LOLs of clever angels.

Incidentally, if I ever become a drag queen, my name would be Man of Green Gables.

The Top Seven Canadianity Drag Names

Peter Womansbridge

Mann Arden

David Suzuk-she

Wayne Gretzkshe

Lloyd Robertsdaughter

Shania . . . mreallyaman

Tammy Hunter

As far as the Confederation Bridge went, the only downside was for nosy people like me who wanted to know, the second someone returned from away, "Whodja see on the boat?" "The boat," of course, referred to the ferries at each end of the island, one to Nova Scotia and one to New Brunswick. Lifelines to the rest of the world.

"Whodja see on the boat?" was a standard Island greeting to someone who'd just come back from a vacation on the mainland. Not "How was Boston?" or "Is your mom still in the hospital in Halifax?" *Whodjaseeontheboat?*

"Well, I seen Socks MacDonald. You know Larry and them. He's Larry's wife Treena's cousin's step-uncle. They live out where the Esso used to be. They were over to Cape Breton for a cribbage tournament."

If you want to fit in on PEI and not seem like an "off-Islander" (someone from away, as opposed to someone from the Island who has gone bad), the appropriate response to this information is:

Yeah (while exhaling).

Yeeeeah (while inhaling).

Yeah (exhaling again).

So Maritimes, the need to establish a link. Maybe the bridge is just a metaphor for our desire to connect. Or mine, anyway. I'd be lying if I said no one had ever called me the Town Crier as a nickname.

Another side note: my sister Marj knows a guy whose nickname is "Come, Come, Whoa" because he works parking cars on the ferry. Lots of people have nicknames on PEI that are usually as a result of one incident decades ago. Just ask her other friend Shitbox, who fell into a kitty litter box when he was two or three, some fifty years ago.

Perhaps my favourite PEI vernacular applies when two people are dating, they're going out, then say they break up and get back together. On PEI you would say, "I heard yaz are going back out!"

Going back out. Extra points for the plural of "you" being "yaz."

We were a Brady Bunch family. My dad had three kids from his first marriage, and my mother had one. I was the caulking that held it all together for a relatively brief time. The proud product of their convenient, if a little ill-conceived, union.

My mother is the daughter of a druggist from New Glasgow, Nova Scotia. He died before I was born, but mostly what I heard about him was how much he adored his wife, so I guess I get that from him.

My dad was from Cornwall, England, and left home when he was fourteen to join the Merchant Navy. He travelled all over the world as a navigator in the forces, and that's what eventually brought him to PEI. He had his own real estate company that he ran out of our house in Sherwood.

He died in 1980 when I was eight, but please don't feel bad for me, bahds. First of all, it was a really long time ago and I have plenty of fond memories with him. Second, the hardest part of the whole thing was adults looking at me with sad eyes. The "Are you okay, dear?" look. That actually made me feel worse, like my life was somehow worth pity.

It also seemed like such a weird way to use energy, making the adults around me feel better about what had happened. If I was born a host, though, as the "running to open the toddler gate at the top of the stairs when people arrived" anecdote suggests, I put those making-people-feel-comfortable skills to the test early on.

There are two things I get from my dad.

One is real estate. I'm addicted to it. One of the first things I do in any new place is score a real estate guide to see what's for sale and what things are worth. Realtor.ca is one of my favourite websites.

Not sure why the price of a "charming fixer-upper in the West End of Winnipeg" is of interest to me, but it is.

The other thing I get from Patrick Torrens is my hyena-like cackle. I've always been a little sheepish about it, and I suppressed it until recent years. My laugh is unnaturally high and staccato. Maybe because of my line of work, too, my default response was always to say, "That's funny" rather than actually laugh. As if I'm dissecting how/why it made me laugh rather than just reacting to it in the moment.

But my wife, Carole, and our girls make me laugh a lot. Taggart does too. So I do it now, more than ever, and so many *TnT* listeners have mentioned how happy my laugh makes them. I love that. Maybe I'm too old now to worry about how it sounds, or maybe it's just that I'm genuinely happier in my life than I've ever been.

Plus, my laugh takes so much energy, I could never fake it.

Childhood in Sherwood, PEI, was idyllic. It was a short walk through the field to get to Sherwood Elementary. On warm summer nights, we stayed out playing until the street lights came on. And we played a lot of hockey—on ice at the Sherwood Sportsplex in the winter and on the street all year long. My world ended at the end of my street, and as a kid I was so fine with that.

Shirts-off Party

Taggart

PEI is a beautiful place. It's the birthplace of nice. A charming and witty island of true bahds. I've not been there near enough, but I hope to have it be a regular stop on my retirement skid. Boy, summers there would keep a geezer horny for life.

I went to my friend Adam Campbell's wedding there a few years ago. It was in a classic farmhouse not far from the Rodd Brudenell River Resort, where I was staying with my wife, Lisa. Adam played hockey and was good bahds with Sean Avery, who was also my roommate during the stint in Los Angeles. Adam played junior hockey with a lot of good bahds, so you can imagine how the wedding reception was.

You don't see keg stands at wedding receptions often, but when you do, you should probably expect a mandatory shirts-off party. These keg stands were long and tall; everyone was trying to make a point on each. You see, it's not that easy to do a rip on a keg upside down for ten seconds. It comes up ice cold and fast, like a 9.79-second Ben Johnson whistling down your throat. It's tough.

Everyone was doing keggers. Young bucks and old folks alike. It was controlled and fantastic, though. I mean, some people got really banged up, but the mood was so fun, it didn't get out of hand or dark. I got up and sat in on the drums and tore it up for good times.

I'm not much of a dancer. I just find it tough to let go on the dance floor without part of me laughing its guts out at my sad movements—even though Drake has seemingly made the "dancing of a fifty-five-year-old man with a game-leg" style acceptable. I somehow ended up shaking it in the middle of the floor with Lisa, and all of a sudden NHLer Danny Carcillo comes right in front of me and yells, "Shirts-off party!" He reached for my fancy new dress shirt and ripped it open like the Hulk. Buttons flew around the dance floor, and wild-eyed Danny went in search of the next victim. I don't think any guy had a shirt on after five minutes. Classic.

The next day, we went to the beach. The hardness of the ocean and the sun blasting on that red sand really stoked the fire of my love for PEI. Jonathan was lucky to grow up in such a heavenly spot. Those rock-hard winters build up some mean humble pie, though. I'll never forget those pictures of the snow from 2014–15. Holy boats! It was piled higher than the houses. I can't imagine having to go upstairs to get out of my house. Heavy Canadianity, bahds.

Dallas, We Have a Problem

Torrens

 One March break in 1981 my mom took my sister and me to Houston to visit a friend of hers. You know how on family vacations you're allowed to get one thing? I saw my one thing the second we got off the plane. It was hanging in the window of a gentleman's haberdashery in the Houston airport.

A white three-piece suit—the kind J.R. Ewing wore on *Dallas*.

My mom did the right thing by suggesting there might be other things that I'd see over the course of the week that I might like better. A Houston Astros batting helmet, say. Or a souvenir from a water park.

Nope. I had to have the suit.

All week long I resisted temptations for other toys and stayed committed to the snazzy suit. On the day we were leaving, we headed to the airport early so that I could be fitted properly for it.

I wore my white J.R. Ewing suit only twice. The first time was singing "If I Was a Butterfly" in front of a sizable crowd at

St. Dunstan's Basilica in Charlottetown. It was even recorded for Cable 10, so I suppose technically that was my TV debut. The second time was the next day at school, where a random game of dodgeball picked up at recess. Turns out a red, PEI-muddy ball left quite an impression on a stark white suit. Over and over again. And the mud stains from my slippery escape attempts didn't help either.

Tide was no match for PEI mud, and that was the end of the suit.

Fortunately, that summer I went to England and got a full Buckingham Palace guard costume with the big black furry hat. Even wore it home on the plane.

My best friend, Mark Howlett, lived across from us. We played catch for hours in his backyard and golf in the field behind the school. Mark's dad, Cecil, was the provincial lawn bowling champion for a couple of years running and even had the big trophy to show for it.

Together with a third friend named Joel Cormier, we had a street hockey team called the JMJs. Joel. Mark. Jonathan. Get it?

On a few occasions, we'd invite other teams from the neighbourhood to come over and play against us. One day, Mark had the genius idea to hide Cecil's lawn bowling trophy in the long grass sprouting out of the ditch beside the "rink." If we won, we'd make them stand on the "blue line" and witness the presentation of a huge lawn bowling statue they didn't even know they were playing for. We'd raise the trophy over our heads in elation. Then pump up the ghetto blaster. Platinum Blonde, "Doesn't Really Matter," cued up and ready to go.

Kid heaven.

Matt Mayhem on Canada Day

Taggart

PEI is also the place where Jonathan and I first met. OLP was playing a show there, and we grabbed some dinner and then went out after the show. We cruised around Charlottetown, trying to find a spot to hang out and have a couple drinks. We couldn't find anything that was open, so we ended up wandering around neighbourhoods to find a rowdy house. That worked like a charm. It wasn't long before we heard a house just raging!

We walked in, and it was so packed that there was no way people would think we were crashing the place. There was a band playing, and people were in every room, having a blast. We went into the kitchen to source out some suds, and we ran into Matt Mays and some other musician bahds.

The party really picked up when we decided to hit the instruments for a gas and to repay the fine folks for the libations. I think we played a bunch of songs by the Band, which is one of my favourites to jam out on. The only issue was that the drums were set up left-handed, and I'm right-handed. "Whatev-salad" is what popped into my mind. I call myself a professional, so I must adapt. So I crushed many Band tunes pretending I was left-handed, and it worked pretty well.

A true good time was had, into the wee hours of the morning. So much fun. People started getting pretty banged up, so it was time to get back to the hotel and call it a night. I wish I knew about the "monkey nuts" that Jono has since spoken about on our podcast.

I would have crushed a dozen of them. I love chicken balls. It reminds me of being a kid fighting for them after a Chinese food order on a Saturday night, elbows firing into my brothers' sides to get a couple more into me. Not to mention hearing the locals saying "monkey nots" over and over. I need that in my life.

Torrens

I remember that night. I'd actually gone to PEI for Canada Day with Mike Smith (Bubbles from *Trailer Park Boys*) because I was interested in/infatuated with this girl named Carole, who said she was heading over with a group of her friends. OLP was playing, and the Hip too. Turbo-Canadianity lineup. To show my true love strong and free I was even wearing my "I Heart Gordon Lightfoot" T-shirt.

So Smith and I met up with the OLP boys at a lobster joint after their show, and before long Taggart and I were volleying good-natured disses back and forth about who each other looked like. He called me Jack Wagner, the soap star who was also a one-hit wonder with "All I Need." I called him Father of Confederation D'Arcy McGee.

We had a great night. Even bumped into Elisha Cuthbert from *Popular Mechanics for Kids* and her boyfriend—some guy in a tight T-shirt named Dion Phaneuf—but I never did track Carole down. She somehow missed my calls, and texted me when she got back home safely to Nova Scotia. She was playing hard to get. I countered with hard to want.

Spoiler alert: We've been married for almost ten years and have two kids. I'm still infatuated with her, and she still doesn't always return my calls.

Patrick Ledwell

To help us cast a wider net for hot tips, we've asked local legends across the country to be Bahd Ambassadors.

On PEI, it's Patrick Ledwell. He's an author, observational comedian and live performer who's got maybe the best take on what being an Islander truly means. Hyper-specific to the PEI experience, yet somehow universal—the mark of a great artist. Here are some of Patrick's suggestions:

My wife, Tara, and I like to do a "burn and earn"—let the inner antelope out for some cardio, then graze a carby table. These are Island burn-and-earn pairings we've actually done, suggesting PEI still exists in the winter too, which it actually sometimes does.

- Call the **Pinette Raceway** in southeastern PEI and go on a rip all afternoon, riding the sulkies on the oval. Classic. No one designing an experience here. Then, go to **Rossignol Estate Winery** in Little Sands, and stick your red-caked nose into as many tiny sample cups of their fruit wines as they'll serve you. Big head next morning, but worth it.
- Walk the boardwalk around **Victoria Park** in Charlottetown, any time of year. Beaut of a harbour, and you'll overhear enough to know who should be running the province, who should be in jail and vice versa. Probably don't cut through the woods after twilight, or you'll catch some Pokémon you weren't planning on.
- Charlottetown bats above its weight per capita in good places to

eat, maybe because of the culinary school. But here's a tip: follow where the old people eat, like, regular. Because they think they're on a tight budget and have so much time to complain among themselves, it makes TripAdvisor look like a bunch of crybabies. So go to **Papa Joe's** on University Avenue, and get the special, whatever it is. All about value.

- I hear Summerside has an indoor trampoline park, and a good restaurant called **OpenEats** that shakes it up with cow heart and lobster ice cream. Sounds like you want to hit the trampolines first.

- Get storm-stayed at **Mill River Resort** in the winter, up west. Sounds a bit "banjos," but shut up and listen. Get some **Vinny's** pizza into you. You don't survive as a rural independent pizzeria unless you know your shit. You'll get to meet people, play shinny, have a drink and then drink the stuff they make. Get someone to take you out at night on the Ski-Doo trails if you don't have a sled and don't fixate on life expectancy. You can learn a lot about yourself, holding on for dear life to a strange man's waist in a screaming Canadian snow.

- Cavendish is famous (ask Jonathan about living in school buses for a summer). But Rustico, down the road, is the year-rounder. Get on your bikes at the national park in Cavendish, maybe at the old **Rainbow Valley** fun park, which the national park bought and removed all the damn sketchy magicians and fun fake owls from. Bomb to Rustico through the park trails, go to **Gallant's Clover Farm** and pick up some mayo, iceberg lettuce and white bread. Get a pound of pre-picked lobster at **Doiron Fisheries**, and eat sandwiches with your feet dangling off the wharf. Jebus wept.

A Tourist (Lobster) Trap

Torrens

Islanders have a love/hate relationship with tourists. Mostly love because they drop a whack of cash on PEI every summer. I know this for a fact, because for two summers while on hiatus from *Street Cents*, I sold T-shirts on the boardwalk in Cavendish at a place called Christopher's Beach Club.

That's what I did during the day. By night I hosted karaoke at Thirsty's Road House—a place that's now a Chinese restaurant called the BoardWok. Ahh, even typing it brings a smile to my face. I love myself some solid wordplay.

Most Requested Karaoke Tunes at Thirsty's Road House in 1990

"Summer Nights" (*Grease* soundtrack)

"Hold On" (Wilson Phillips)

"Bust a Move" (Young MC)

"U Can't Touch This" (MC Hammer)

"We Built This City" (Starship)

"Don't Worry, Be Happy" (Bobby McFerrin)

My preferences were more designed to make audiences shift uncomfortably in their seats, like "Wicked Game," "Crazy for You" and "Private Dancer."

"Wicked Game" might be the greasiest/horniest song ever. Any time it comes on, it makes me feel filthy, no matter what I'm doing. Mowing. Driving. Digging in the garden.

If you've listened to the poddy, you'll know that I like speaking with a Québécois-Franglais accent. It was there in Cavendish that I studied it hard. So many Québécois tourists, often doing little to combat the stereotypes. Wearing Speedos in restaurants, smoking in stores, using words like *tabernac* and *câlisse* at the price of touristy tank tops. But I love Quebecers. And they love the beach on PEI.

Americans too, who often did *their* part to keep the stereotype alive. They enabled me to hone my sarcasm.

"We'd like to have dinner in Calgary. Can you give us driving directions?"

"Sure. Turn left and just keeeeeeep going. Can't miss it."

Taggart's Top Five Canadian Bands

As Torrens mentioned, we bonded on PEI at a show Our Lady Peace was playing with the Hip. I've been lucky over the years to share the festival stage with some unbelievable acts.

What makes a band great? For me it's influence, experience and skill, honesty and integrity. These provide a common thread among all great bands, but maybe even greater when it comes to Canadian bands. Here are my Top Five!

5. **Sloan**

    They are the perfect example of a great band. They have been through it all together from the start. They've had so many hits, and are still producing great songs. I think of Sloan as the Ramones of Canada. They are very connected to what's right in music. They didn't quite get the support in the States that they deserved, and I feel their songs should be heralded more world-wide. The songs on their first records still stand up as classic pop/rock jams, and they still maintain that great energy on songs today.

4. Blue Rodeo

I can't get enough BR into my soul. Such a great band. They always worked their asses off and ground out one of the best followings in Canadian music. Thank God for songs like "Hasn't Hit Me Yet" and "Lost Together." Those jams help people like hospitals do. Curing the blue feelings of the day like master doctors. So good it hurts, they strike deeply into the glory of Canadianity.

3. The Guess Who

How can I not go to Burton Cummings and the boys? How can I not think of Burton Cummings when I'm in Winnipeg? You just do. The chance of spotting Burton at Salisbury House or the track? I'll keep on trying until it happens. Then I can shake that man's hand. Seriously, they were so prolific for a good stretch of the '60s and '70s. So many great songs. It's unreal when you go down the list of how many there are and how diverse they were. They had shit-loads of hits south of the border too. They should be in the Rock & Roll Hall of Fame in Cleveland, if you ask my opinion. Some of the best tales I've ever heard involve Burton or Randy Bachman. So classic.

2. The Band

I can't go a week without craving some Band. They're so good I can hardly explain it. A style that can't be traced—the most original band that ever was. So great that they couldn't be copied. So great that Bob Dylan *had* to have them as his backing band. Four-fifths Canadian, but Levon was a pretty incredible American. A stew of talent that soars above everyone with ease. So much musical talent that bands would retire after seeing them play. No hints of arrogance, but sharklike ego. You couldn't match their musical prowess. The sound of their harmonies is like a happy hug from your parents after a big life event—the birth of a baby, or a funeral. So thick and warm. Nobody heals you like the Band. You could cure a bad day in seconds with one of their tunes.

The brashness of Rick Danko, such a rebel and tough as nails. The softness of Richard Manuel, a deep and soothing soul who got lost in his darkness. The genius of Garth Hudson, the epitome of what a teacher should be. The cunning of Robbie Robertson, the barnacle on what's cool and hip, scheming and manipulating like a comic book villain. And of course, Levon Helm, the wise sage who knew everything, the how-to master. He was the leader and the man who steered the ship into the most important waters. Shit, he even quit the band when he got booed during the Dylan electric tour of 1965. He went and worked on an oil rig! Talk about getting away. When he came back, he directed them into the "Brown Album." That Civil War–feeling rock, the halftime ruggedness. So good. So Levon. Maybe the bahd of bahds in my opinion.

The Band was huge and had major internal strife that eventually ended it. What a run, though. Canadianity at its finest. Thank you, Ronnie Hawkins, for putting these guys together. You created a monster!

1. The Tragically Hip

When I was a teenager, I spent a lot of time in a small brick room at Rumble Fish Studios by myself, skipping school to practise drumming. Eventually I was thrust out of Emery Collegiate and ended up writing my correspondence-course assignments in that grey, empty space while taking breaks from practice, playing along with tons of old records by bands like Zeppelin, Cream and the Who. The Tragically Hip was one of those bands I was into. I played along with all of their records.

When I got to see them at the Ontario Place Forum in 1989, I really thought they were incredible. I have so much fun watching them. So many songs that pound you with great memories for hours. It was an honour to do shows and eventually become friends with all of them. I respect them immensely and love how they do business in music.

When I heard about Gord's cancer, it was a real gut punch. It was like hearing about a family member getting sick. You feel the weight of all those memories from so many different points in your life, growing up with the person. The way those shows on their last tour went down and the love that was created is something that no Canadian will ever forget. The way they've been through it all together as a band from day one, all the ups and downs without anybody getting canned or leaving, the Tragically Hip is the best Canadian-true-and-true band ever.

REALtor or FAKEtor

Torrens

As I mentioned, my dad owned Torrens Real Estate on PEI. It's not just the listings I'm low-key obsessed with, it's Realtor photos too. Like, who told him to wear that sweater, or why is her neck straining at that odd angle? On *Taggart & Torrens*, we play silly games all the time—including this one, REALtor or FAKEtor.

See if your bahds can figure out whether these are real real estate agents or fake real estate agents.

1. **Cash Sales, HomeLife Realty**
2. **Kyle and Kendra Killkenny, Killkenny's Kuality Homes**
3. **Sherlock Homes, Century 21**
4. **Judy Ball and Greg Ball, Bowes & Cocks Limited**
5. **Mac Meanoffer, Royal LePage**
6. **Gary Lake, Lake's Lakefront Estates**
7. **Lee Jeans, RE/MAX**
8. **Mort Gage**
9. **Su Casa, ERA Real Estate**

REALtors: 3, 4, 7 and 9. FAKEtors: 1, 2, 5, 6 and 8.

Y2K? Y Not!

Torrens

In 1999, the CBC asked me to be a correspondent in Charlottetown for their Y2K coverage. As someone who's always had a secret fascination with news and news anchors (remember Stone Phillips?), I was psyched! To get to be on the roster for what was technically a news production in my hometown on this big occasion was a dream come true.

Peter Mansbridge is one of the original bahds. He's razor sharp, charming and funny. Still, when any major event breaks out in the world, there's no one else's calm, informed voice I'd rather listen to. So, naturally, he was helming the CBC's coverage of such a monumental event.

Remember, they weren't sure if bank machines would work or if the world would end as 1999 rolled over to 2000. The Atlantic Time Zone was one of the first in Canada to cross over, so this PEI post was prime real estate.

I debated what to wear. It was New Year's Eve, but it was also news. I wanted to look competent but informative, classy but casual, so I opted for a navy turtleneck (class) with a Helly Hansen foul-weather reflective parka (news). In hindsight, the parka might've made me look more like an airport baggage handler than a news guy, but whatever.

In my head I'd scripted a lyrical love letter to my home province and planned to blow people away with just how articulate and newsy I could be right out of the gate.

"Colleen, come look at *Jonovision* on the news. Ever good!"

The day arrived, and it was gloriously sunny. My first hit was to be with Mansbridge, in midafternoon in front of Province House, where the country was formed. Kind of a "set the scene of what we can expect" double-ender.

In my mind, my hit would go like this: Peter would tee it up from the studio in Toronto and throw it to me, nodding and smiling confidently from Charlottetown. Then I'd say my piece.

"Peter, tonight the eyes of the country turn to its birthplace, PEI, the little island with the big heart cradled in the waves of the Atlantic Ocean, where tonight some fifteen thousand people are expected to descend in the downtown core to ring in this new year and, indeed, new millennium."

How newsy does that sound? Instead, here's what happened.

As expected, Peter threw it to me by saying something like, "We go now to Charlottetown, where Jonathan Torrens is standing by. How are things looking there, Jonathan?"

And I said this: "Petel . . ."

That's right. I called him "Petel." I choked on Peter Mansbridge's name. He laughed, as you would. I was rattled, but I forged on.

It ended up being a great day, for Canada and for budding correspondents. Bank machines still worked after midnight. Peter was, as always, incredible in both stamina and wit, and even I had my moments. A highlight was interviewing a 103-year-old woman who'd been alive for the turn of the last century. When I asked what she hoped to do that evening, with a twinkle in her eye she said, "I wouldn't mind meeting a man."

Mansbridge . . . now *that* would've been a good name for the fixed link.

PEI Gotta Do's

POUND a Beach Chair Lager frosty soldier at Prince Edward Island Brewing Company.

CRUSH an egg roll and some monkey nuts (sweet-and-sour chicken balls) at Canton Cafe. (**Torrens:** A mainstay of my life since I can remember. Anyone who's going to the Island, I tell them to have an egg roll there, and they scoff. Then they call me—while it's still in their mouth—to thank me.)

DESTROY a bowl of chowder at the Merchantman. Chef Loo's game is tight.

NAIL a quick lunch-and-shop combo at the Dunes Studio Gallery.

PASS OUT at the Great George Hotel.

CRASH a play at the Victoria Playhouse. A charming little theatre in an even charminger (that's a word, right?) little town by the sea. Drill some chocolate from Island Chocolates a few doors down.

JAM at Harmony House Theatre in Hunter River. Beautiful venue, run by a couple of bahds, Kris and Melanie Taylor.

WHEEL some road rockets on the patio at Peakes Quay in the summer.

KILL some baked goods at Leonhard's, a great breakfast spot in Charlottetown.

DEMOLISH some raspberry pie from Prince Edward Island Preserve Company in New Glasgow. But save room to . . .

SHOVE your way into New Glasgow Lobster Suppers! Crowded and touristy, yes. But you get a bib and fresh homemade rolls with your buttery crustacean companion. Go late to avoid the blue-hair bus rush!

JUMP off the bridge with the locals in Stanley Bridge, a short drive from the madness of the Cavendish Boardwalk. Bridge jumping is kind of a tradition on the Island. Deep water and a sandy bottom make for ideal conditions. Hey, Sandy Bottom is a pretty good name for a cross-dresser too!

HOOVER some fine dining with the inn crowd. Inn at Bay Fortune (Chef Michael Smith) or Inn at St. Peters—can't go wrong with either. The food is rivalled only by their respective views.

Ontario: Lakes, Rivers and Bahds That Give 'Er

Bahd Bands

The Arkells (not just because drummer Tim Oxford pieces together the poddy but because they rock harder and better than just about any other band in Canada right now)

Blue Rodeo	**Metric**
Russell DeCarle/Prairie Oyster	**The Parachute Club**
Donovan Woods	**Rheostatics**
The Tragically Hip	**Steppenwolf**
Barenaked Ladies	**The Darcys**
Triumph	

Five Notable Bahds

Given the size and population of Ontario, this could easily be fifty.

Graham Greene. We know what you're thinking—not another "audio technician turned Academy Award nominee story"—but Graham's Oscar recognition for his work in *Dances with Wolves* was nothing short of historic.

Phil Hartman. Arguably the most versatile utility player in the history of *Saturday Night Live*. A man of many voices, faces and impressions. Crushed it on *The Simpsons* and *NewsRadio* too.

Samantha Bee. Took her stint as the longest-serving correspondent on *The Daily Show* during Jon Stewart's reign and parlayed it into a sitcom deal and talk show at TBS. Almost impossible to believe she wasn't even considered for the desk after Jon Stewart left. Smart, saucy and not afraid to call it how she sees it.

Rachel McAdams. Has obviously achieved international acclaim for roles in movies like *The Notebook* and *Wedding Crashers*, but keeping it Canadian with her performance in the critically acclaimed *Slings & Arrows* = bahd.

Trish Stratus. This bahd-ass retired wrestler has parlayed her fitness-model beginnings into a whole other business: Stratusphere.

The Good Ol' Days

Taggart

Being a young kid in Canada was pretty cool for me. I spent my first five years in Toronto, but the next nine (the important ones) spotted around southern Ontario. The most special place being Mansfield. It's a tiny town. Imagine rivers and swimming holes, lush hills and valleys that mimic nursery rhymes. It was a magical place to grow up. A place where outside beats the shit out of TV and video games. I still remember how strong the urge to get up and out of bed was. The mad singing of the cicadas in the trees hypnotically summoned my brother Jetsun and me outside. Hide and seek crushed, while tag took on a whole new level of fun with all the trees and hills. We would catch crayfish and get snipped by snapping turtles in the Boyne River. We would go swimming in Greer's pond, not before hearing Mrs. Greer throwing out the cynical "You can go swimming, but don't get wet!"

Winters were incredible there. My eyes hurt thinking about the bright sun blasting off the snow. Snowbanks became small buildings that bordered the subdivision we lived in. Snow days were often— pretty much every time a reasonable storm blew through. We got at least one or two a month in winter. I loved hearing about big storms. I knew I'd be off the next day, partying hard outside all day. The only bummer was my dad had to drive to Toronto for seven thirty every morning, so that meant he had to shovel out and drive slow, and would be late coming home from the rough roads. Seven thirty is early for anyone, but especially for drummers like Ronnie and me. On the upside, he used to bring home toys that were damaged from Sears—he worked in the maintenance department of their Rexdale warehouse. I loved it when he came through the door with a box full of slightly broken trucks and other goodies in his arms.

Willie Nelson aptly recalled these moments of his own youth as "Good Times." Mansfield was all about these. Four TV channels were all we had—we grew up on CKVR in Barrie, TVOntario (now TVO), CBC and a slightly fuzzy CTV. Shows like *Leave It to Beaver, The Andy Griffith Show* and *The Beachcombers*. And on TVO, kids shows like *Readalong, Passe-Partout* and the classic Sol on *Parlez-Moi*. So much Canadianity on TVO. We got our sense of humour from *SCTV*. How lucky were we to have such a great group of hilarious people? I remember staying up and watching Brian Johns (Eugene Levy) talk about money, and still remember seeing Levon Helm play "Summertime Blues" on *SCTV* like it was yesterday.

It's funny. We only had a few channels, but there was always something worth watching on TV then. Now I have two hundred channels and I'm taping *Seinfeld* reruns because there's nothing else to watch! I'm not sure if my brain is too stimulated, or if TV is just full of formulated whatnot. Maybe I just miss the simple and stupid shows like *The Silver Basketball* and *Harrigan*. You can't recreate that numbness you'd feel after watching shows that seemed like everyone involved was just winging it, hoping the sets and costumes would save the script. Canadian TV was better when it had shades of embarrassment, in my opinion. Or perhaps it was just a more acceptable type of embarrassment. Less ego and more of a humble fail.

Whatever it was, I sure do miss it.

Ontari-OMG, This Place Is Huge

Torrens

Ontario is a sumbitch. Almost too big to comprehend. It's bigger than Texas and bigger than France and Spain combined. To understand how big it is, you really have to drive it.

It's vast, yet dense. Like Fox News.

When I first went "up to Toronto" to work on *Jonovision*, I felt like a combination of Barney the Big Purple Dinosaur and Crocodile Dundee. I'd smile at everyone I passed on the street and say good morning to commuters sitting across from me on the subway. It turns out that's not how most people act in the Big Smoke.

Remember, I grew up in Charlottetown, where there was a Subway gang, but it was only called that because they hung out at the Subway sandwich shop.

Here's the thing, though: the people I met and worked with who were *from* there were so nice. Exceptionally so. It's almost like the people who move there from smaller towns act the way they think you're supposed to act in a city, versus the way city people actually do. As if new Torontonians are trying on Big City the way kids try on their dad's ill-fitting sports coat.

Sometimes I think Toronto gets a bad rap, and I feel like I too never gave it a proper shot. Whenever I was there for work, I always had a house back east and would head home the second I was finished whatever I was doing. So I never really lived there so much as I just stayed there.

Every weekend, I'd get in my truck and drive as far as time would allow. Didn't matter which direction—Orangeville, Omemee, Orillia. I'd go as far as I had to for a Tim Hortons drive-thru. I'd crank *Gord's Gold* and take in some farmland. Brick bungalows and farmhouses, which I hadn't really seen much before. I loved those drives. Wide-open spaces always left me feeling recharged. Still do.

Growing Up with Ronnie

Taggart

When I was four, we lived in subsidized housing in Rexdale, Ontario. It was a pretty rough neighbourhood and there were plenty of "warmongers"—the term Dad used for any wrongdoer over a certain level of decent human etiquette. A person only looking to cause harm or get into trouble.

My dad loathed these types; they would get his blood boiling and cause him to erupt to a Pompeii-like circumstance.

Dad used to take the bus to the bicycle shop where he worked at that time. He was quietly waiting alone for the morning bus when a group of kids with hockey sticks ran up to him and beat him to the ground, bloodying him up. They continued to hit him all over his body before running off. Dad collected himself and stumbled home. He had open gashes all over his head, bruises and cuts on his arms, legs and torso. Just shit-kicked. He went to the hospital for stitches and bandages.

What an ordeal for a man with four young kids and a shitty job. This was a new low for my dad's confidence. He felt these kids had taken away all his dignity as he walked to the bus stop the next day, his body covered in all these bumps and bandages.

Alone again, waiting for the bus, and the fucking kids come back again! Sticks in hand, running in for round 2 with Ronnie, except this time Dad's gasket was blown before he heard the second foot-step of the warmongers. He reached into the garbage, fished out a pop bottle and smashed it onto the sidewalk, reached down with both hands and swooped up a pile of glass. He threw it into his mouth and proceeded to chew it up whilst screaming about warmongers and how he'd been waiting all his life for them, and this was a time they wouldn't ever forget. They all scattered away like my dad was a sign of the apocalypse.

Dad went to work happy that day, knowing he had regained some control of the situation. All those stupid tricks, like breaking glass in your mouth without getting cut, he picked up in the Bronx with his gang, the Junior Bacooches. A handy little trick, I'd say.

He ended up using it again ten years later in Mansfield. Some stupid neighbourhood warmongers were tearing up our grand-parents' lawn across the street and staring at my dad while he was mowing the lawn. Never stare at my dad. He walked over to the car—the kids were drinking from stubby beer bottles, so it was around 1983. They were all banged up and yelling at Dad. They threw a bottle at him from the back seat, it sailed just over Dad's head and broke on the ground, and you can guess what happened next. The old double-handed swoop and rip into the mouth for a good chew. He then walked towards the car, not unlike the cop in *Terminator 2*, real easy and slow-like. The kids in the car were stunned and frozen. I should mention that this was a smaller Datsun-type shitbox, so Dad reached with both arms to the roof of the car and began to rock the car back and forth with these four kids in it like it was a Power Wheels toy. The thing was just bouncing and the punks turned into pussies, all crying and screaming. They screeched away, bouncing, almost running my dad over in the process. Dad came in the house like he had just been doing some extra chores. He had that same sense of accomplishment anyway.

Snow Business

Torrens

The first long gig I had in Toronto was for a CBC kids special called *AIDScare/AIDsCare*. It was a sketch comedy show about the myths surrounding AIDS. Think about how crazy that sounds. This was early on, when people still thought you could catch it from a toilet seat.

I was the host, Sue Johanson was the sexpert and rapper Snow was the musical guest. His single "Informer" was at the top of the charts and he was a big "get."

It was also a big break for me. I was still on *Street Cents*, and this was my first network special. The number of cameras was a little intimidating, but fortunately the on-camera stuff always came fairly easily. Someone gave me a great piece of advice early on. Al MacPherson, a warm grandfatherly cameraman at CBC Halifax, told me when you're looking into the camera, pretend you're talking to someone you know, love or have a crush on. It'll give your delivery a warmth and casualness that it wouldn't have otherwise. It was easy when I was talking to Al's camera. He was such a bahd.

We shot *AIDScare/AIDsCare* in the Masonic Temple, the big, beautiful building that would later become home to MTV Canada and *Open Mike with Mike Bullard*.

My friend Richard Mortimer wrote it (we'd already worked together on *Street Cents*) and a woman named Lynn Harvey produced it. She was a very accomplished variety producer, and the three of us would soon after team up on *Jonovision*.

One of the *AIDScare* bits involved me dressing up as a life-sized penis (typecasting?) so that Sue Johanson could put a tire-sized condom over me, as a way of demonstrating how to do it properly. The costume was something to behold. It had a ceramic head (with a cutout for my face), a flesh-coloured onesie and brown fuzzy slippers to represent the pubic mound.

Sue is a wonderful woman, but not tall. In order for her to properly pinch the tip, I had to lean over to one side rather flaccidly. This created a curious silhouette, but it was still a very effective demo for the age group of our target audience.

The week leading up to the live taping was going well. We were banking some great sketches to roll into the show. Everyone was proud of the work we were doing and very excited for Snow's arrival. He and his bodyguard Too Tall (not his Christian name, I don't think) were coming in from Jamaica on Thursday, and the show was shooting in front of a live studio audience Friday night.

Thursday evening, Snow arrived on schedule and went to his hotel to settle in. When he left the hotel for the sound check, he left his room key at the front desk and said that he wouldn't be back. Maybe the room wasn't up to snuff, maybe he planned to stay with friends. In any case, he left the distinct impression that they wouldn't be seeing him again.

After sound check, he and Too Tall left in a van with a CBC driver to go hang out with some friends. It must be quite a feeling to be back in your hometown with a #1 song on the charts.

Then, late in the evening/early in the morning, they decided it was time to crash. But where? Snow had left his key at the front desk. Fortunately, Too Tall still had his, so they went back to the original hotel and up to their room—which was, by now, someone else's room.

Imagine your surprise if you were asleep in your room when Snow, TooTall and a posse of partiers burst in unexpectedly. For obvious reasons, security became involved, and later the police as well, who ultimately arrested Snow . . .

The night before our show.

That was Part A of the story. Here comes Part B.

On show day, we continued to rehearse and prepare as though everything would be fine. We finished dress rehearsal, having left a hole for Snow's performance of "Informer." Meanwhile, Dee Gilchrist (a production executive at the CBC) was working her magic during Snow's arraignment to get him freed. "But Your Honour, he's here to perform at a comedy show about AIDS for teenagers."

We flicked on the Citytv news between the rehearsal and the show, and there were Snow, TooTall and Dee running down the steps of City Hall on their way to the Masonic Temple! Just in time!

The show started. It was going well despite the fact that there was no Snow. How unusual as a Canadian to pray for Snow—lololollolololololololollllin.

I got dressed in my penis costume, the bit killed and the kids loved Sue. I walked off stage as Snow was about to walk on. We had pre-taped my intro of him, so I wouldn't have to introduce him in my penis costume. A CBC publicist grabbed me and said, "We need a quick picture with you and Snow." I said, "Cool, I'm just going to change real quick . . ."

"There's no time. This is our only chance to have a promotional pic of the two of you together."

Snow and TooTall were leaving the building as soon as his performance was over. So I sighed and stood beside Snow, trying my best to smile as the photographer offered suggestions. "Snow, put your arm around the penis. Penis, put your head on Snow's shoulder."

For what it's worth, he could not have been more of a gentleman. Friendly, accommodating, kind. He saw the humour in the situation better than I did.

Somewhere in the bowels of the CBC in Toronto, there are press pictures of Penis Me and Snow. Chart-topping rapper Snow, giving the peace sign with his arm around a dickhead. I keep meaning to get my hands on one, blow it up and get it framed.

I saw him again years later at a bar in Toronto. He'd become friends with Mike Smith and was still the same awesome dude. We had a great chat about songwriting and he shared his strategy, which is that the best songs all have a nursery rhyme quality. Interesting philosophy.

And you can't tell me "Informer" isn't a dope-ass jam. *Still.*

For the Love of Drums

Taggart

Drums mean a lot to me. I knew they would be part of my life even before I could play them, almost a "Yeah, I'll get to it" kind of deal. I felt a connection with them from the moment I touched a drumhead. I'll never forget—it was in Grade 3. A kid from high school came to my school and played some beats in an assembly at Mulmur-Mono, near Shelburne. He played like "Wipeout" or "Sing, Sing, Sing." Either way, it blew my mind. I was a drummer. I knew it. The calm, the cool.

Drummers are like goalies or even golf course superintendents. They are a little bit different. They affiliate with all walks of life. Drummers tend to not care what people think. We just want to play. We don't care about needing the listener. We know that if you're good enough, that shit doesn't matter. We connect with time. We disappear into it, and try to affect the feeling of it. Pushy or laid-back, or right in the middle. What you hit in the backbeat makes the feeling.

Even though I was all in after seeing that kid play in assembly, I just had a feeling that I would delve into drumming like a madman someday, but not yet. Maybe it was the fact that my dad was through with drumming himself.

I'll never forget the sound of drums being destroyed in our basement in 1979. At four years old, I was far too young to understand what was going on, but I remember the smashing and banging. It was New Year's Eve, and Dad had no gig. He lost it. He quit drumming professionally. His closure needed an exclamation point, and that meant destroying all his gear. Holy boats, what a sound. It was a true finisher. He came upstairs from turning everything to dust and never played drums again.

So I grew up not seeing or hearing drums at all, with the exception of the kid at my school assembly. Dad would show us rudiments like double strokes and paradiddles, but it was casual and nobody really took it anywhere further in the house. It was always far in the back of my mind to play. I was so into baseball.

Flash forward to Barrie, Ontario. I was fourteen years old and I had just got home from school. I was in the back parking lot of our apartment building on Innisfil Street. I looked on the pavement beside the car and saw a taped-up pair of drumsticks. All broken, but repaired with greasy clear tape. I picked them up and got really horny at the idea of becoming a drummer all of a sudden. I marched upstairs to talk to Dad, I was so fired up. I came up to him, sticks behind my back, and told him I wanted to learn to play drums and showed him the wretched set of sticks. His faced soured and he said, "Why would you wanna do that?" with an angry, beaten feel.

"I like it, it's cool, Dad," I said with absolute fear. He responded, "Well, if you're gonna do it, you should be the best, or don't bother."

Well. That was good enough for me. I figured I'd give it the same go as I had with baseball. I was ready for the challenge. Dad started giving me lessons on everything he could help me with. He made me a practice pad out of foam rubber taped tightly around a book wrapped in a towel. Classic. I had to wear out that pad before I could even think of getting a drum kit. I burned that pad up for three months, and there was a huge hole in the middle of the surface. Time for a drum kit!

I looked in the *Buy & Sell* newspaper and found an ad for a small Ludwig kit and cymbals for 250 bucks. I was so excited, I bugged my mom for days 'til she finally caved and we went to get the drums. The guy selling the kit had it in his garage. He opened the door and showed my folks and me the drums and cymbals. My dad was cracking up at how shitty they were. They were made up of scraps of random kits. They all had Ludwig decals screwed into them, but they were mismatched and brush-painted black. Just horrendous. The cymbals were basically tin toys—all small and thin, black and spotted green flecks. Basically, the worst drum set in history.

I had to have them!

I just wanted to play some beats. I didn't care that they were the worst drums ever, even though they totally were. We somehow never even got a deal. We still paid $250. The guy must have sensed my desperation. But I was over the moon. I couldn't wait to get home and set them up.

I Tried Degrassi (But I Didn't Inhale)

Torrens

Not saying I'm responsible for *Degrassi: The Next Generation*, but I'm also not saying I'm not. Okay, I'm probably not. But . . .

During *Jonovision*, we often asked viewers what they'd like to see on the show. Over and over again, kids suggested a reunion of the original cast of *Degrassi*. It had been a few years since we'd seen them in *Degrassi Talks* (the way-ahead-of-its-time discussion show aimed at high school students) and there was a curiosity about the now-twentysomethings.

Quite quickly, our story producers found and booked Joey, Snake, Spike, Stephanie Kaye, Arthur, Yick—the whole band was getting back together! We began putting some feelers out, cautiously optimistic that it could happen.

When people heard we were doing a reunion, they freaked. Fans from as far away as San Francisco booked flights to come and be in the audience. There was so much to talk about that we decided it would be a special two-part episode.

So the legend goes, there was so much buzz around the episodes that Linda Schuyler realized there might be life left in the franchise after all those years. She pitched *Degrassi: The Next Generation*, and the rest is TV history. It may well have already been in the works, but I still like to pretend I had at least something to do with it.

A few years into *Degrassi: The Next Generation*, they wrote a two-part season premiere in which Emma (Spike and Shane's now-fifteen-year-old daughter) discovers that her dad isn't a doctor as she'd been told all these years. In fact, he's a patient at a mental hospital.

You might recall that, in the original *Degrassi*, Shane took acid and jumped off a bridge. In the storyline, he was in a coma for several weeks and was left with significant physical and mental disabilities.

Billy Parrott, the actor who played Shane in the original series, didn't want to reprise his role in this fashion, so they were stuck with a two-episode script but no dashing blond actor to play the role.

Enter me. That might be the most uncomfortable sentence I've ever typed.

Not sure if it was thanks for hosting the reunion or the sheer fact that I was a blond actor about the age Shane would've been when the episode was filmed. In any case, I was asked to play Shane McKay and instantly said yes. What an honour!

I accepted before reading the scripts and had second thoughts immediately afterwards. Not because they were badly written— they were great. It's just that I wasn't sure I had the acting chops to pull it off. It was, after all, a pretty dramatic role on a show known for high drama.

This was the story: Emma is feeling left out because her mom, Spike, is expecting a baby with Snake. Emma sneaks away from school to go and look for her dad, and she finds him pacing in a tiny room. She struggles with whether to pursue a relationship with her dad, who wasn't quite the romantic figure she'd always been led to believe.

Here are the other clues in the script about Shane MacKay, post– unspecified brain injury:

1. He's easily upset.
2. He rocks back and forth and knits to calm himself down.
3. He speaks with a debilitating stutter.

Fortunately, all-time great Bruce McDonald (check out *Highway 61* for serious Canadianity) was directing the episodes, and he's the loveliest dude. Gentle, kind, encouraging.

The episodes—both the TV ones and my character's violent ones—turned out very well and I'm really happy that I did it. Proud, even. If you're ever looking for ways to crush a lazy Sunday afternoon, it's worth a Google.

So there you go, bahds. Solid Canadianity right there.

Great Moments in Canadianity

Megaproducer (and father to Tori) Aaron Spelling was aware of *Degrassi* and liked the idea of doing a show about teenagers going through real issues. Linda Schuyler met with him about the possibility of doing an American version of the show.

She explained that one of the reasons viewers so identified with *Degrassi* is because the kids looked real. The creator of such sexy and stylized shows as *Dynasty*, *The Love Boat* and *Charlie's Angels* didn't think the "real-looking" thing would fly, so he went on to make his own high school show, *Beverly Hills, 90210*, starring BC native Jason Priestley.

The End of Baseball

Taggart

As I got more into the drums at age fifteen or sixteen, I got less into baseball. I was tired of the grinding politics with coaches and parents, the pecking back and forth between parents and coaches, the clash of different classes of the parents of the players. It got thick and tiresome for me. Maybe it was the constant daily practice in between team practices. But the game hardened for me with the repetition and technical view I had drawn of it. All this stuff was turning me right off the game. I was done with ball, and all I wanted to do was play drums.

Just as things were getting horny for my baseball opportunities! I was invited to come out for an Atlanta Braves training camp in Toronto, a chance to be looked at by the legitimate scouts and trainers of the Atlanta Braves. My mom drove me there, and as we rolled into the park I couldn't believe the number of kids that were there. I was legitimately into not getting out of the car and rolling back home. I felt it was a no-chance situation for me.

My mom wasn't letting me get out of this, though. She was right there for every step, scoring every game from my squirt days. She told me to get the fuck on that field, and I got out of the car. It was a plethora of kids, I'm gonna say hundreds. Almost every one of them was taller than me. Some of them were seven feet tall and covered with hair. The group was made up of the best players from all over southern Ontario, and me—a five-foot-nine seventeen-year-old confronting the Monstars from *Space Jam*. Some of these guys were already throwing in the nineties! I topped out at eighty-five and my love for the sides of the plate.

I ran, hit, fielded, ran, caught, bunted, ran and pitched for what seemed like hours. After the tryout I spoke to a couple guys with browned potato-chip faces about my future. They spoke highly of my accuracy and the movement on my curveball. The only junk I had. They said I could maintain good contact at the plate, and they would like to see me at another tryout that would give me a chance to go into their farm system. Maybe score a sweet free boat ride through a swank school with a scholarship.

There was something weird about that experience—maybe the validation from the chip guys, maybe seeing giants with far more strength than me play the game with ease. All I know is that my passion for baseball was left on that field, or maybe in the parking lot. I didn't want to touch a baseball unless it was for shits and gigs. Which was a bummer, because my disassociation from the game included no longer watching major league baseball on TV. This happened in spring of 1992, bahds. I screwed myself out of both Jays World Series championships! I was fairweathered and pissy with the Jays for a few years. Dumb, eh?

Canada Day in the Capital

Torrens

One summer during the off-season from *Jonovision*, I thought I would volunteer as a driver on the CBC Canada Day show. It's quite a spectacle when a hundred thousand Canadians gather on the front lawn of Parliament Hill to celebrate.

It's also usually hot. Like, change your shirt four times a day hot.

My first job was to drive a cube van full of cold drinks from Toronto to Ottawa. I love driving, and this was a fun adventure for me. The plan was to drive up with the drinks and drive back with some set pieces that were made in Ottawa to store in the CBC art department's lockup. That was quite a place, as you can imagine. Props and sets from *Air Farce*, *Wayne & Shuster*, *The Tommy Hunter Show*. I loved to go down there and wander the aisles, trying to spot recognizable items.

Anyway, this particular week was unseasonably, unreasonably cold for Ottawa. Like, hot chocolate in late June cold. All this to say my cold drinks didn't exactly fly off the shelves the way they normally would. The production had to instead buy a bunch of coffee and tea to try to warm up the crew, who were manning and womanning their outdoor positions for hours on end during this freaky frosty snap.

At the end of the week, not only did I have all the set pieces in my van, but also all the cold drinks that no one ended up consuming. My li'l rig was way overweight by the time I left Ottawa for Toronto.

Now it makes sense why kids in passing cars were pointing and waving at me. It's not because I was a trucker, offering a friendly toot in passing. It's because my axles were bent and my wheels were like Bambi on ice.

I pulled into a truck stop in Belleville and drivers literally came running out, pointing and laughing. Turns out the axles were seconds away from snapping on the 401. Oops. I had to ditch some drinks and switch cube vans to get back on the road.

That wasn't the only misadventure that week.

I was driving Paul Brandt and his band back to the hotel after their dress rehearsal, and one of the guys asked what the plan was for the night. I told them my mom was a lady of the evening in town and I could make arrangements if need be. I thought I was being funny, but they did not. Things were very quiet and uncomfortable for the rest of the drive. In hindsight, without the proper context, I can see why that might've been off-putting, but discomfort has always been something I've found pretty funny.

And I got lost with Buffy Sainte-Marie. Like, sweat trickling down the back of my neck lost. Buffy had exactly one hour to get from the Hill to the recording studio, lay down two lines of a song and get back in time for rehearsal. The studio was eleven minutes away. Tight, but doable.

She hopped in my seven-passenger Windstar, sweet and chatty. I started driving. And kept driving. Twenty minutes. Twenty-seven minutes. There was forest, and water, but no studio. No GPS—only one-way streets taking me farther and farther from civilization. It got to the point where there wasn't even a way I could have her back to the Hill in time. I had a stomach ache from the sinking feeling that I'd really screwed up.

At one point, Buffy stop talking and turned to me with a furrowed brow. "Uh, can I ask you a question?"

Here it comes. "Sure."

"What astrological sign is your cat?"

Phew. She couldn't have been more of a total pro. That seems to be the case, though. The ones that have been around for a while are generally pretty cool. It's the insta-stars that can go from zero to dicksty in a hurry.

Want me to blow your #Canadianity mind? Tom Green was a story producer on *Street Cents*. We met when he was producing a story I shot in Ottawa. Can't remember what it was about now, but I do remember that it ended with my mother pelting me with tomatoes while I was dressed in a garbage bag.

I maintain that Tom's only problem is that he's way ahead of his time. Always has been. I remember when he was outfitting his entire house with cameras to live-stream a TV show on the internet several years ago. It seemed so crazy. But he was right.

From Nowhere to Everywhere with the Drums

Taggart

After a couple of years of getting heavily into drumming, I was looking to find a real gig. I felt that I needed to get some firsthand experience playing drums professionally after taking lessons from a variety of incredible drummers, like Rick Gratton, Paul DeLong and Vito Rezza. Those guys were already making their mark in a huge way as drummers in Canada, and I wanted to be like them so badly.

I was already hunting for gigs at sixteen, taking any audition or jam opportunity there was. I was hanging in greasy clubs, learning the ropes of the true pro musician. I would sneak around with my friend Joe Iannuzzi, an outcast like me whom I met at Emery Collegiate. I met him in a loner stairwell. I think I had a Zildjian T-shirt, and he was tapping his knee with a set of sticks. We hung out together a lot, both aspiring to become jobbers in drumming. We were heavy drum nerds.

I ended up being out most nights and skipping school for practice, eventually getting booted out of Emery for missing class. I would hide in my parents' closet until everyone was gone, then roll over to my rehearsal spot and play drums 'til midnight. When I had no school left to attend, I opted for correspondence courses. I had a small room with a drum set and stacks of essays. Play all day, hang with all the working drummers, like Mike Siracusa, a protege of Vito Rezza's. Mike would let me watch his various gigs and occasionally let me sit in. I learned a lot from him. He's a total bahd.

I would always pay attention to the local musicians-wanted ads, looking for auditions, and would frequently try out for bands or cover gigs. I was completely cognizant of the fact that if you want to be a professional musician, you shouldn't expect the stars, you should know that it might just be pubs, hotels and cruise ships, which is the reality for most musicians.

I was prepared for the grind. My dad knew it all too well, having been a Toronto jazz musician in the '60s and '70s. He wasn't very pleased with my new life path and goal of following in his footsteps. He told me of the hardships of choosing music as a way of feeding your family. Long hours and little pay. He looked at it as a waste of time, but he also knew of the urge to follow your instincts and respected my choice.

One day I came across an ad in the back pages of *Now* magazine for a band that was looking for a drummer. It was near my house, too, in the Weston and Finch neighbourhood. My mom drove me to the studio space on Toryork Drive, an area more noted for chop shops and Sicilian neckties than music. A pretty greasy neck of the woods. When I finally got into the studio, I saw a bunch of dudes coming in and out and it seemed like it was gonna be a quick audition. I took quite some time to set up my kit, which gave us a chance to talk a bit. Mike (Raine hadn't adopted the new handle quite yet), Chris and Mike were all in their mid to late twenties, so I felt a bit stupid at seventeen, with my baseball windbreaker and, likely, bad shorts or cords from the '80s.

I finally got my kit set up and we just started jamming feels. It felt very easy and interesting. I knew there was a pretty good chance they would ask me to join. It wasn't just that we had good communication through our instruments; my being young and so eager to play drums was obvious to them. They asked me to join a week or two later, and we started work on *Naveed* right away. It was hard work and a lot of play, hours of working up parts and hours of Wiffle ball.

I really enjoyed the early days, not just because of the early success and fantastic tours, but because I was just growing up at the same time. Being in buses and planes, ripping around all these crazy shows with Page and Plant, the Ramones, Faith No More. That was my high school. Picking brains of other drummers, learning and offering information. I remember seeing Trilok Gurtu in New York City in the hotel lobby. Trilok is a legend! Such an incredible drummer and percussive genius. I was talking to him about his work with John McLaughlin and Joe Zawinul and telling him how he was a badass. A great chat.

I felt I probably would never see him again. Then I happened to run into him twice more. Both times in Los Angeles. The last time, he even threw out a "Hey Jeremy! How are you?" and when I said I was great and asked him the same, he responded with "Slammin'!" Such a bahd!

It was great to see all these people who had been my heroes growing up, being so nice and down to earth. I learned so much about how to be a positive person by seeing these legends spending hours of extra time with fans or anyone that came into their space. Being a bahd goes a long way.

Once OLP started to get serious traction, I think my parents and family enjoyed it even more than I did. My dad was super-happy that I got off on such a strong foot. He's always been awesomely proud. My mom used to track our radio and MuchMusic play. She knew all the charts. She'd call into stations and request us. Just classic. She'd call me, all pissed off, saying, "Aw Jer, they're tryin' to keep ya down on 102! I only heard you once today!" So great. They got into my music career the same way they wanted me playing baseball. They were happy just for the reason that I too was happy.

The Perfect Storm

Torrens

 During *Jonovision* I was on a date with a girl who worked at the CBC. I suggested we go for Greek food on the Danforth. I'm sure that, to a kid growing up in Toronto, foods from other countries aren't that exotic. But growing up outside of Charlottetown, food from anywhere other than China or the sea still felt so exotic to me.

We met at the restaurant. She looked cute in the candlelight and we chatted easily while we ate several dishes.

She drank wine.

And I drank milk.

I'm not sure why. Milk isn't something I drank a lot of as an adult. But on this night I drank a lot of it. I'm going to guess, conservatively, two litres.

Hummus.

Milk.

Taramasalata.

Milk.

Spanakopita.

Milk.

We stopped at Blockbuster to rent a movie on the way back to her place. She really wanted to see *The Perfect Storm*, with George Clooney and Mark Wahlberg. As we roamed the aisles, the perfect storm was beginning to form in my stomach. Turns out oil and milk go together like oil and water.

By the time we got to her sea-monkey-sized basement apartment, tiny beads of sweat had formed on my forehead and I was really struggling.

During the opening titles, I turned up the volume on the movie and excused myself.

Her bathroom made an airplane bathroom look roomy. I had to do-si-do around the door to get it closed, and she was lying on the couch mere feet from me.

During the first "outburst," I coughed to try to drown it out. During the second one, I ran the tap. Then I turned on the shower. Then the tap as well.

Then I ran out of toilet paper.

After fifteen minutes or so, I was okay to leave, so I stood up, washed my hands and opened the door a crack.

But I wasn't quite finished after all.

So I slammed the door and turned the tap back on. I was light-headed from such a sudden and aggressive purging. All I could think was "Get me to my truck." But what could I possibly say to her? It was already too late to save face, and I assumed a second date was out of the question.

Forty-five minutes later, sweaty, exhausted and mortified, I opened the door and stood as tall as I could. She was lying on the couch, pretending to be asleep.

"I guess something didn't agree with me," I casually mumbled under my breath, making a beeline for the door.

I often imagine her telling that story to big groups of friends, and the punchline is "Guess who it was . . . friggin' *Jonovision!*"

Early-'80s TV and MuchMusic

Taggart

When I lived in Mansfield as a young kid in the early '80s, you couldn't get cable. You had the small handful of southern Ontario channels, and that was it. Unless you had one of those *Sputnik*-sized dishes in your backyard. My grandparents, who had recently moved in across from us, had one. Those things were epic. Hundreds of channels and open feeds, all with the touch of a huge dial that would send the massive dish revolving with a grinding hum. Visiting across the street to the calm and collected house of my grandma and Papa Doug was always a treat. My grandma was always very strict and strong-minded and Papa Doug was the most organized person I've ever known. PD had a tool area in the garage that looked like a working military shop, dialled to the max with places marked for every piece, small or large. Tip-top.

Their house was always immaculate, so you had to play by the rules or you were out. Fuck up a few times and you were on Grandma's shit list, and once that happened, you were doomed to stink-eye. Even worse, Jetsun and I fucked up enough to never get to go on the family trips to Britain but had to sit through countless hours of my brother James and sister, Jenni, on vacay in the UK with Grandma. Jenni climbing Stonehenge, James trying on one of those bearskin hats from the Queen's Guard cats. Both our other cousins, too! Haha! Fraser pointing scarily into Loch Ness, Elliott climbing Hadrian's Wall.

Even though we never got to go overseas with Grandma, we still loved her and thought she was the bomb. My sister, Jenni, moved in with Grandma and PD shortly after the satellite installation—a great move, if you ask me. She became pretty hip, watching MTV and HBO all the time. I remember back then, "Weird Al" Yankovic ruled the land. It's truly uncanny how long that guy has been successful by ripping up artists with his odd charm. Loads of Weird Al, the Police, Huey Lewis and Dire Straits. Given the success of MTV in the US, it was only a matter of time before Canada had its own musical television franchise.

When MuchMusic launched in '84, I was aware of *City Limits* on channel 57, which was the CHUM-owned Citytv, a station I could get up in the sticks of Mansfield. Christopher Ward would play great music videos, interviews and even comedy sketches. Mike Myers made his TV debut there with his Wayne Campbell character, doing reviews with that classic Scarborough accent. *City Limits* was a shrunken version of what MuchMusic became. John Martin, creator of the Citytv show *The NewMusic*, and Moses Znaimer, a co-founder of City, put MuchMusic on the air August 31, 1984. It's obvious that there was a massive young Canadian audience just waiting to bite on a twenty-four-hour-a-day music and culture channel. City was already producing great shows like *The New Music* with J.D. Roberts and Jeanne Beker, John Majhor's *Toronto Rocks* and Ward's *City Limits*, to name a few.

By the time I was living in Cookstown, outside Barrie, I had cable and the opportunity to watch MuchMusic on the reg. I've heard many stories about how crazy that building got with partying in the '80s, but that goes for any radio station or TV production back then. There are also crazy stories about radio stations Q107 and CFNY back then. Par for the course, I suppose. Seemed like everyone was getting banged up in that decade.

I remember seeing Peter Garrett of Midnight Oil on Much a lot. MO and Crowded House seemed to be the international fave bands that Much supported. Not surprisingly, it gave both of those bands lucrative Canadian fan bases that churned tickets for years.

Much started breaking bands big time. By the time I was in OLP, I knew it was all about getting on MuchMusic. I saw right before my eyes the difference between getting love from them and dying a slow death from not getting played on Much. They were a huge part of OLP's success. It provided a band with direct access to every kid from thirteen to twenty-five. You could guarantee your record was going gold—possibly platinum—if you got three singles in heavy rotation. Then your live audience multiplied, and if you were a good live act you could pack theatres on the strength of a run on MuchMusic. If Much put you under their microscope, you felt the difference real quick. I remember having never heard of Moist, and then seeing them every twenty minutes on Much. After that, they were ramming halls. It happened all the time back then. The connection Much created with its audience was incredible.

Those guys basically created a branch of the Canadian TV tree equally as important as *Hockey Night in Canada*. The advertising dollars grew to staggering levels, while the savvy young hosts got paid squat. The influence of MuchMusic grew too. The MuchMusic Video Awards, for example, went from bands setting up in closets around the Much environment amidst clouds of hairspray to two city blocks getting shut down, two weeks of stage construction and massive corporate support. Bands might not break on Much anymore, but it still wields a big sword with the teenyboppers, and if you're a young band, you will still see a jump in awareness.

I always enjoyed the people who worked there, from the first time I did an interview. It was with Erica Ehm, and I was eighteen and shitting myself inside. Seeing people that you grew up watching is pretty weird, but when they're nice, it makes it way cooler. It was a pleasure to be accepted by all the bahds who have come and gone through those doors at 299 Queen Street West, from Strombo to Craig Halket, and Amanda Walsh to Master T. All bahds!

Ontario Gotta Do's

DESTROY blueberry pancakes at the Senator. Just a block or so from Massey Hall, between the Eaton Centre and Ryerson.

PEEP the view of Niagara Falls, the Thousand Islands or Point Pelee National Park.

HAMMER a hike in the Hills of the Headwaters, in Melancthon.

CRUSH some grapes in the Niagara region or Prince Edward County.

POUND the white water at Wilderness Tours Adventure Resort in the Ottawa Valley.

PITCH a tent in Algonquin Provincial Park.

SHARPEN your blades and skate the Rideau Canal in Ottawa.

EXPAND your mind at Stratford's Shakespeare festival.

FREAK your freak at Science North in Sudbury.

JAM some history at Sainte-Marie among the Hurons in Midland.

DRILL some BBQ at the Memphis Fire Barbecue Company in Winona.

DEMOLISH a pizza at Maker Pizza in Toronto.

HOOVER a burger at Chuck's Burger Bar in Hamilton.

SWANK it up at Eigensinn Farm in Singhampton.

BANG your head at the Danforth Music Hall in Toronto.

New Funswick

Bahd Bands

In-Flight Safety

Eric's Trip

Chris Colepaugh

Grand Theft Bus

Roch Voisine

Matt Andersen

Matt Minglewood

David Myles

The Motorleague

Five Notable Bahds

Donald Sutherland. Kiefer's dad. Pretty decent actor in his own right.

Louis B. Mayer. The co-founder of movie studio Metro-Goldwyn-Mayer grew up poor in Saint John, the plucky son of resourceful Russian immigrants.

Ron Turcotte. Thoroughbred racehorse jockey.

Sir Samuel Leonard Tilley. Father of Confederation. Supporter of the Intercolonial Railway. Also widely believed to have suggested "Dominion of Canada" as a name for the new country.

Winnifred Blair. The first Miss Canada.

Moncton + Fredericton = A Ton of Fun!

Torrens

I have to confess something, and I feel very weird about it. I didn't always "get" New Brunswick.

Let me explain. As I mentioned, when I was growing up on PEI, there was the fear that Moncton people might come over and ruin the place. Also, my impression of New Brunswick was formed by yearly weekend trips to Champlain Mall for back-to-school shopping. If you spent time in a mall in Moncton in the late '70s, you'd have a strange impression of the place too.

Plus, when I was eight I took the bus/ferry over to Moncton every Sunday for guitar lessons, and I encountered some strange characters on the walk from the music teacher's apartment to Pizza Delight, where the bus picked passengers up.

As I got older, New Brunswick was the "we're not quite on PEI yet" portion of the trip from Nova Scotia. Then, years later, it was the "almost home from Ontario/California" portion of my drive. Not fair. I didn't give New Brunswick a fair shake, with its covered bridge, Covered Bridge chips and bilingualness.

So I'm late to the NB party, but now I'm very happy to be here. Turns out New Brunswick is rad and I was the one who was missing out all these years.

If you ever doubt that Canadianity is a thing, check out Canada Day at Captain Dan's in Parlee Beach. It's on full display on the colourful front lawn of the Algonquin Resort in St. Andrews by-the-Sea in fall. It's in Plaster Rock during the annual World Pond Hockey

Championship, where 120 teams from all over the globe compete to have the best time of their lives.

It's certainly in the party atmosphere of downtown Freddy Beach, where Taggart and I found ourselves hosting the FredRock Festival a couple of years ago. Check out these headliners:

. Hey Rosetta!
. Joel Plaskett (whose first band, Thrush Hermit, wrote and recorded a *Street Cents* theme)
. Blue Rodeo

I say all the time that Bruce Hornsby is my ride-or-die music chick. He's been riding dirty with me for many of the big moments of my life, both happy and sad. I didn't realize just how much Blue Rodeo's been there too. I learned this from seeing them live again after a few years.

Not unlike with New Brunswick, it took seeing Blue Rodeo up close to cement just how much I loved it. On a warm summer night, they played long and sounded great, triggering all the powerful, where-were-you-when musical memories.

They say the world is divided into Lennon people and McCartney people, and similarly you have to choose between Jim Cuddy and Greg Keelor. All I can say is that I wanted to be both that night as they traded licks and hits on a relentless set list that included "Try," "Hasn't Hit Me Yet," "'Til I Am Myself Again," and "Diamond Mine." Cuddy. Keelor. Cuddy. Keelor.

I don't know that I've seen an audience more rapt, more willing to sing along with every word.

They saved "Lost Together" for their final encore and invited other bands up to sing. Taggart went up and shared a mic with Greg Keelor, who even asked him if he knew the words to the third verse! Isn't that crazy? Keelor was going to let Taggs sing the whole verse. How bahddish is that? Never know when that kind of knowledge will come in handy.

We went back to Fredericton on our Comedy & Canadianity tour and played Vault 29. It was the last show of our tour, and there were probably 250 bahds there, having a ball. There was a pond hockey team that had just won a tournament that day, and they called themselves the Bahds. They even gave us official Bahd jerseys.

See? New Brunswick is *rad*.

East Coast Seafood and the Stones

Taggart

Jonathan can attest to the number of fish-related meals I try to fit in when I'm out east. When in Rome, bahds. The pile of lobster the caterers brought in for the Rolling Stones' Magnetic Hill show in Moncton in September 2005 was six feet high. An absolute mountain of it on ice, with an alien-sized barrel of melted butter. It was enough to be opening for the Stones for the third time, to meet and have a quick chat and get a picture with them before they were whisked onto the stage, enough to hear Mick say nice words about OLP as they started into "Tumblin' Dice," but that fuckin' lobster and melted butter, bahd. It was all about that experience of crushing a plateful or three of that glory.

What a production that show was. They had dozens of semis and hundreds of people working for them—such a large stage to set up, they had a second full production crew that was already in the next city, because it took days to build. It was like they threw up Liberty Village in Toronto in three days. So big! They had group tours going around, looking at the Stones' equipment onstage. Not a meet and greet, just a tour of their shit up close. These people were paying thousands of dollars for this. That's when you know you're big, eh? Holy boats. I mean, it's pretty cool to see first-edition amps, priceless guitars and worn-out drums, but to throw down a couple K to look at it? Whatev-salad.

My Afternoon with the Donald

Torrens

 It used to be harder to drive through NB before the highways were twinned. You could get stuck behind a big rig for several hundred kilometres of woodland, with nothing to think about but how much money the Irvings must have from owning all those trees. Not to mention the gas stations. Not to mention the taquitos that they sell at said gas stations.

The Irvings aren't New Brunswick's only Royal Family. One-third of the world's french fries come from Florenceville-Bristol—home to the McCain family empire. McCain is also known for those ridiculously tasty Deep 'n Delicious cakes. And the punch that made Roberto Alomar a household name.

Saint John, New Brunswick, is home to Moosehead, Canada's oldest independent brewery. It was founded in 1867 by Susannah Oland and is still run by the Oland family to this day. Chances are pretty good you've pounded some of their fare into your wordhole on a hot summer's day. Though locals would probably recommend Alpine.

Saint John is also home to Donald Sutherland, for my money one of the greatest actors in the history of the craft. His onscreen presence is captivating. His eyes are piercing. His voice is equal parts soothing and terrifying.

When I was in California, my friend Lynn was producing the Canada Day special for the CBC. It was a big show in Ottawa every year, and the great challenge is to make an annual event seem especially memorable. She came up with the idea of getting Canadian superstars to sing the national anthem, and she would cobble the performances together into an impressive montage. Since I was in LA, she asked if I'd go with the camera operator to field-produce two of the singers: William Shatner and Donald Sutherland. Obviously, I was in like Crocs.

Shatner's part went as expected. He was firm but fair, business-like but brief. Then we packed up and left for our arranged meeting place with Mr. Sutherland.

When we'd traded emails, he asked where we should meet. Being relatively new to LA, I first suggested one of the only landmarks I knew: the entrance to the Santa Monica Pier. Seeing as it's maybe the biggest tourist attraction in all of LA, that's exactly where you *don't* want to meet if you're Donald Sutherland, for so many reasons that are clear to me now.

Fortunately, he owned a property not too far away that was vacant at the time, and he suggested we could meet there for some privacy.

We arrived at the appointed time. The gate swung open. As we were gathering our gear, I suddenly felt the coolness of a shadow, and I turned to see Donald Sutherland standing behind me, all eight feet of him, backlit by the harsh California midday sun.

"Hello," I said.

Crickets. He smiled but said nothing for what felt like an eternity. It was probably four seconds. He'd already started to turn when I heard . . .

"You can set up upstairs."

The camera dude and I looked at each other. Were we supposed to follow him?

We did, and I took the opportunity to quickly give D-Suth the once-over. Not only was he tall and commanding, but his long hair was whiter than the moguls at the Calgary Olympics in '88!

I followed him up the stairs and offered, weakly, "You know, I'm from the Maritimes."

Silence. Did he not hear me? Should I have not spoken? Why was I ever even born?

"Oh yeah? Whereabouts?"

I told him. He listened, genuinely interested, and introduced us to his wife, Francine, who is lovely and French-Canadian and charming. We set up in the most beautiful vacant space I'd ever seen in my life.

As the camera guy was setting up, Donald told me this story about Saint John (I'm paraphrasing, but the gist of it was something like this): During the Second World War, towns and cities in the Maritimes were debating whether they should have a lights-out curfew just in case bombers were going to target them. After much discussion, the town council in Saint John decided the hell with it. Might as well leave the lights on, because if a bomber flew over, the crew would probably assume the town had already been destroyed.

Donald Sutherland is funny AF.

He then sang the anthem in his beautiful singing voice, in both official languages, in one take.

They thanked us for our time and we went downstairs to pack up. As the cameraman was putting gear in the trunk, I got in the passenger seat to write some edit notes while they were fresh in my head.

Suddenly, I was in shadow again. I looked out the passenger window and all I could see was a lengthy thorax. It was Donald. He put his hand on the window, and I thought it must be some kind of Hollywood greeting, so I put my hand on the window to touch his, like you would against the glass at a prison visit.

No, he gestured. Put the window down.

Oh.

Only problem was, the windows were electric and the cameraman had the keys. Hard to explain that to someone's midriff through a closed window. It suddenly felt very hot in the car, so I pushed the door open, and in the process moved Donald Sutherland back.

Guess what he wanted?

To invite me to a screening of a film he'd made the next day in Santa Monica.

You can take the bahd out of the Maritimes, but you can't take the Maritimes out of the bahd.

New Brunswick Gotta Do's

SCOPE Hopewell Rocks. It's kind of a two-fer, because the experience is totally different at high and low tide. Give yourself time to experience both.

CRUSH the Boar Poutine at the Tide & Boar Gastropub in Moncton. Parm-encrusted haddock is another solid move too. And brunch there is tight.

TAKE A RIP into the Saint John City Market or Fredericton Boyce Farmers Market. Both are friendly and fun destinations.

POP into the Imperial Theatre. Musicians will tell you that this Saint John gem is one of the nicest-sounding venues in the entire country. Doesn't matter who's playing, just make sure you take in a show there.

VAS-Y to the Village Historique Acadien in Caraquet. If you're into history, get a taste of what life was like as far back as 1770.

Nova Scotia: Rum & Cokers and Practical Jokers

Bahd Bands

Sloan

Joel Plaskett

The Trews

April Wine

The Stanfields

Wintersleep

The Rankin Family

Ashley MacIsaac

Natalie MacMaster

Ria Mae

Port Cities

Jenn Grant

Rain over St. Ambrose

Five Notable Bahds

Anne Murray. Belongs in the Bahd Bands section, yes, but deserves special recognition for the fact that she's sold well over fifty million records worldwide. Keeps it low-key these days, in typical Canadian fashion. To get an idea of just how good a singer she is, try singing "Snowbird." You can't.

Classified. Doesn't front, pretending to be something he's not. Raps about what he knows—fatherhood, being from the East Coast, living in the country. Solid lyrics combined with a keen ear for samples. Only going to get bigger. Does a lot of good for a lot of people on the side too.

Ellen Page. This Oscar nominee hails from Halifax and got her start on local fare like *Pit Pony* and *Trailer Park Boys* before *Juno* changed everything. A terrifying tour de force in *Hard Candy*. Changed lives with *Gaycation* on Vice.

Nathan MacKinnon. On this list not only for his mad skills on the ice but also for the grace and humour with which he handles being the second-most-famous NHLer from Cole Harbour.

Sidney Crosby. Won some gold medals, a couple of Stanley Cups, a world championship or two. But really achieves bahd status for how low-key he keeps it when he's home in the summers. Like, shopping-at-Sobeys low-key. Like, Anne Murray low-key.

There's Lobster Stew and Lots to Do in Halifax

Torrens

My family moved to Nova Scotia when I was twelve, to be nearer to my aging grandmother. Halifax might as well have been New York City to me at the time. Everything felt so sprawling, intimidating and exciting.

I'd never lived in an apartment before. It was a two-storey unit with a wooden spiral staircase in it, right across the street from the Public Gardens. If you've been to Halifax, you'll know that Spring Garden Road is the main drag downtown, and we were just steps from the buzz.

Maybe you've been to a Concert on the Hill on Canada Day, or maybe your ancestors arrived in Canada through Pier 21, as tens of thousands did.

Halifax boasts the second-deepest saltwater port in the world, if you can call that boast-worthy. It also has a small, walkable downtown core and multiple universities, so the vibe is young and energetic.

As daunting as I found the sheer size of it, though, I also quickly embraced the opportunities there.

When I was sixteen, I got a job at the Halifax Lobster Feast. It was an all-you-can-eat lobster buffet on the Halifax waterfront, on a converted Dartmouth ferry boat. For $29.95 you could crush all the fresh mussels, scallops, haddock, chowder, rolls, salad, rice and dessert you could stand.

Most folks would eat one or two lobsters. One night, a gentleman from Texas who weighed close to five hundred pounds came in with his son, who was close to four bills.

We watched in horror as the man ate seventy-nine lobsters, every bite carefully dipped in butter. These were called canners, so they'd be between a pound and a pound and a half including the shell.

His son ate close to sixty.

My boss kept saying, "Get over there and stop them!"

"How?"

"Offer them some rice pilaf or drop off warm rolls!"

Nothing doing. These hustlers were all about lobster in their gobsters. We watched helplessly as they sunk us, with their buttery chins shining in the candlelight.

Early Atlantic Touring with OLP

Taggart

One of my earliest experiences as a touring musician was a cross-Canada tour opening for 54-40 in 1994. They were and still are a great band, and they always treated us amazingly.

They were touring their *Smilin' Buddha Cabaret* album, a tribute to a legendary Vancouver supper-club-turned-punk-bar of the same name that was closed down. The band bought the famous sign and had it onstage behind them. It did create an amazing vibe, but the sign was fucking huge, and arduous to get in and out of some of the smaller club shows on the tour. My best friend, Alex, was helping out as my drum tech, and I had such a blast hanging out with him for weeks.

The eastern Canada run might have been the most fun. I

remember being in Cape Breton at some small upstairs club (probably the biggest nightmare venue for that sign). The place was totally rammed and a sweat box—one of those places where the crowd merges with the band, like an insane house party. I really got a great taste of how wonderful the music fans are in the Maritimes. They get *right* into it. Serious bahds.

What's Your McBeef?

Torrens

I was at St. Pat's High School in Halifax and got invited to audition for this new CBC show for kids. It was a consumer affairs show, based on a British show called *Money Penny*.

I had several auditions and came close, but didn't get the job at first. A kid named Chris did. He was a skateboarder and much cooler than me. It was probably the right decision.

Luckily for me, it didn't work out with Chris and *Street Cents*—or the other way around—and I was hired full time for episode 3 of the first season after doing a Street Test segment in which I ate only fast food for a week. Hardly a stretch, considering that's what most teenage boys eat anyway, plus I worked at McDonald's, where I got a free meal every shift.

McDonald's was actually a very formative experience for me comedically, starting the very first day I worked there. My shift manager asked me to take the french fry rack across the street to the gas station to get the wheels aligned. In my crisp new uniform and so anxious to please, off I trotted across a busy street, pushing the unruly fry rack.

When I got to the station and asked the mechanic whether he could help, he didn't even say anything. He just pointed in the direction of the restaurant. I turned around to see the entire store, employees and patrons, pointing and laughing at me in the window. I'd been had, and good.

They stuck me in the kitchen at first, and I got pretty good and fast at making burgers and breakfasts.

Working the drive-thru was where I got to experiment a lot with where the good-taste line was and what was funny across the board.

One night in particular, the drive-thru was bumpin' and an impatient guy kept asking me to take his order. I was busy and told him politely I'd be right with him.

After thirty seconds or so, he said, *"Take my order, bitch!"*

Well, that wasn't very nice. So I just responded the way anyone else would in the same situation.

"Hold your bird, captain. I said just a second. Is your date being paid by the hour?"

Can you imagine? Some acne-laden, headset-wearing sauce bucket throwing that at you through the drive-thru speaker?

He slammed the car in park and stormed inside, demanding to talk to the kid working the drive-thru, but I was nowhere to be found. Good thing he didn't look in the walk-in freezer out back, where I was shivering and howling.

Another time near the end of my fast food career, I was working the drive-thru one Sunday afternoon when a vanload of Boy Scouts came through. Not sure why exactly I thought it would be a good idea to poke happy faces in the buns of their Quarter Pounders with Cheese. It just struck me as so funny to think of someone opening their burger and seeing it smiling up at them.

Turns out the doughy red-faced Scout leader didn't share the same sense of humour. He parked in the parking lot and marched in, with his little Scout ducklings behind him. He waved me over, held up the smiling burger and asked me if I thought that was funny.

I didn't want to lie. Seeing him standing there, all earnest in his small hat and tiny tie, just made the situation twice as funny to me. I couldn't help it. I answered yes.

It wasn't long after that—maybe around the time that I accidentally crushed several pricey headset batteries in the trash compactor—that my McDonald's career came to an end and my TV career got started.

As far as TV school goes, *Street Cents* was the best possible training ground for a young performer. It was partly a straight hosting gig, delivering information to camera. It was also partly a sitcom, with written scenes and therefore lines to learn. Best of all for me, it was a place to practise and hone impressions. I loved doing characters, from Bob Saget on *Full House* to Don Cherry on *Hockey Night in Canada*.

Street Cents was an incredibly formative time for me. The crew became surrogate parents. The cast became my family. Such a clich-eh, but it was where I spent most of my time as a teenager.

More than anything, I got to travel all over Canada, meeting people and shooting little stories for the Canadian Broadcasting Corporation. It was not a responsibility I took lightly. I saw places I'd never in a million years get to go, and people would tell me things they wouldn't tell their best friends. It was a pretty good fit for a nosy/curious person.

It was also where I met Mike Clattenburg, who would go on to create *Trailer Park Boys*. I didn't go to university, which is where most people find their *people*—like-minded, challenging friends for life.

I'd never met anyone quite like Clattenburg. He had a show on Cable 10 called *That Damn Cable Show*, which was years ahead of its time in tone. I was a fan of *TDCS* and so excited to work with Mike.

Clatty got his sense of humour in part from his father, Ken. When Mike was studying TV at Kingstec (the Nova Scotia Community College campus in the Annapolis Valley of Nova Scotia), he'd come home to work for the summer. Everywhere he went, people would ask how it was going working for Ben's Bakery.

Mike was understandably confused. It came out that Ken had been telling everyone who asked about Mike that he was driving a truck for Ben's, delivering loaves all over Nova Scotia.

Such a non sequitur, but what I loved best about that stuff was the commitment that a joke required, even when you're not around for the payoff. Mike and I—along with Brian Heighton, who played Ken Pompadour on *Street Cents*—became fast friends. It really felt like we spoke the same language. We'd challenge each other to do shocking pratfalls in malls and at the bank. Call Shoppers Drug Mart and try to squeeze the word "mawfucka" into our question. "What time do you mafsks close tonight?"

We tried to jam our brand of humour into the show wherever we could. If you watched episodes from the Clattenburg era, there were definitely early shades of J-Roc. He and I both went to high school with a bunch of dudes who looked, sounded and talked like that, and it made us both laugh.

Clattenburg worked at Sobeys, and there was a tall, skinny kid named Arnold who worked there with him. One day the manager asked Arnold to wash the lettuce and then walked away. Arnold didn't move, and when Mike asked if he was going to do what he'd been asked, Arnold responded, "He ain't beatin' me." Which meant if it came down to a fight, the manager couldn't *force* him to wash the lettuce. Do you guys find that as funny as I do?

We did a *Street Cents* bumper for a segment where my mouth was superimposed over the Queen's face and then we recorded my voice saying "Eyes all over to one side" the way J-Roc would.

One time, we even brought some pre-J-Roc to the Pit. We were testing a product called the Miracle Thaw that claimed it could thaw meat in mere moments or something. As I was throwing the product into the Pit, we changed the line from the standard "We think _____ is Fit . . . for the Pit" to "Go on witcha, Miracle Thaw." Just something about that patois made us laugh. Still does.

Despite the fun we were having making it, at the time there was nothing outwardly cool about the show. It was a kids consumer affairs show on the public broadcaster. It was hardly Sloan getting signed to Sub Pop Records. But for us, to have access to cameras and crew and a national platform was intoxicating.

Several times during those years, I called Ryerson to inquire about the radio and television arts program there. The very patient woman I spoke to always asked why. She told me I was working in a job that lots of their graduates would love to be doing. "If I were you, I'd show up early, stay late, ask questions, take on extra tasks, just be a sponge." I'm so thankful that she was on the other end of the line. What sound advice, and I took it to heart. It's actually great advice for anyone in any career. Mentoring is such an important element for someone entering the workplace, and we've lost it in recent years.

Looking back, I'm really proud of *Street Cents*. It really did empower kids and give them a voice, without talking to them in the condescending manner that its predecessors sometimes did.

Like *Jonovision*, *Street Cents* also gave kids in the regions some insight into what their peers across the country were doing.

It was also where I realized that I'm most comfortable in a hybrid setting. *Street Cents* was a hosted show with parodies. *Jonovision* was a talk show with sketches. *Trailer Park Boys* is a mockumentary. *The Joe Schmo Show* was a fake reality program. Even *Taggart & Torrens* is prone to flights of fancy and surreal moments. I think that's why I like doing it so much.

In the past, I've done some gigs that haven't really felt like me, and I think it's because I've slipped into the character of a game show host instead of being *me* hosting a game show. Being yourself on TV is hard to do.

Jay Onrait and Dan O'Toole can do it.

James Duthie can do it.

Ron MacLean can do it.

Come to think of it, most sports guys are good at it. Through practice, you find your voice and your rhythm, just like drumming.

Taggart's Top Five Drummers

This is a list of important drummers for me personally . It's not a be-all, end-all Top Five. It's the five drummers in the Canadian industry who most inspired my own playing. They are all pretty insanely talented, though.

5. Glenn Milchem (Blue Rodeo and Change of Heart)
    Glenn is a badass. From his early days on the Toronto rock scene to the ease of theatres and arenas with BR, he has always been

one of the most tasteful players out there. Great feel and plenty of chops deep in his palette. I remember he used to crush a double pedal with workboots on. That's classic.

4. **Ray Garraway (Salvador Dream and k-os)**

Ray was the most interesting drummer I can think of. He always had a sticky sense of time, and it was almost impossible to watch him play. He looked like he was about to screw up all the time, but if you closed your eyes it was seamless. Such amazing ideas and concepts. He was a true original. I will always cherish the many days of hanging out, buying records, chatting on the phone and laughing hysterically. I will always miss him. He passed away far too young.

3. **Paul DeLong (studio great)**

I studied with Paul and think he's one of the most precise drummers I've ever seen. His playing is probably most famous from Kim Mitchell anthems like "Patio Lanterns," "Go for Soda" and "All We Are," but his depth in technique in a bunch of different styles is why I had to learn from him. He taught me great Latin grooves and transcribed crazy Vinnie Colaiuta beats from Zappa's *Joe's Garage* album, specifically tracks like "Dong Work for Yuda."

2. **Mark McLean (George Michael, Catherine Russell)**

Mark is such a fantastic jazz player. Incredible time and feel. I love hanging with him to talk about drums and life. I first saw him play when he won a drum competition in 1989 at our local drum shop. We were both fourteen! I always hit him up when I'm in New York. He's as great a bahd as he is a drummer.

1. **Vito Rezza (Joni Mitchell, Gino Vannelli, John Lee Hooker)**

Vito was probably my most important mentor/teacher. He gave me great advice and never held back on critiquing my playing. His ability on the drums is unparalleled, always evolving and pushing every envelope. I always respected his opinion. He never eased up on others, and he always cut right to the point. He is known to get steamed and blow his top. He kind of reminded me of my dad. Maybe that's why I like him so much. It's always a pleasure when I run into him.

Maya and the Gorilla

Torrens

The most Canadian I've ever felt was being drunk on rye at the top of a mountain in the Northwest Territories and coming face to face with a muskox with Rick Mercer. Boy, did he stink! The muskox, that is. In my experience, Rick always smells great.

Oddly enough, the second most Canadian I've ever felt was at a live sex show in Amsterdam with Ken Pompadour from *Street Cents*.

Before I launch into it, you have to know I didn't want to go. I strongly feel my discomfort is essential to your enjoyment of this story.

Ken's real name is Brian Heighton, a great actor and great buddy who instantly became my best friend when I arrived on *Street Cents*. Well, he was *my* best friend. I was probably more of an excited/annoying puppy to him at first, but we grew to be very close.

Brian Heighton is a Renaissance man. Truly. A remarkable painter, great cook, skilled carpenter, phenomenal guitar player, well travelled. There isn't much he can't do. Plus, it was inspiring to watch him play the cartoon character of Ken with such panache.

To nineteen-year-old me, he seemed so worldly. One summer while on hiatus, we took the night ferry from England to Rotterdam and then the train to Amsterdam. The city's rep for debilitating smokables and window-shopping for sex workers is well earned, which is why I was surprised to discover such a beautiful city full of art and bikes and rivers. We went to the Van Gogh Museum and Anne Frank's house and did the Heineken brewery tour.

Sitting under a giant tree, sleeping off a beery lunch, Brian suggested we go to a live sex show.

The truth is, there's nothing really seedy about it. Amsterdam's underbelly is out in the open for you to scratch and pet and use as a pillow if you want. It's just that watching a couple of bad actors bumping uglies was not my idea of the best time.

Plus, *Street Cents* had rubbed off on me (pun intended?), and $75 was a lot of dough to spend on witnessing mechanical intimate relations. Talk about What's Your Beef!

But I couldn't really argue with his "when in Rome" approach, and so I reluctantly agreed.

When we arrived, I was nervous. The show is ongoing, so you pay for your ticket first, stumble into a dark theatre and join the show in progress.

If I didn't feel dirty before we entered, the dozen or so pervy lurkers in yellow raincoats who dotted the theatre really tipped the balance. We found some seats in the second row, much nearer the front than I'd hoped, and Brian sat in the second seat, leaving me the aisle. In hindsight, no one else was sitting up front. That should've been a red flag.

I'll spare you my review of Blackman & Robyn and Popsicle Paula, but suffice it to say it was indeed, as advertised, a live sex show. Not unlike in a magic show, act after act found new and interesting ways to make things disappear.

I was actually starting to enjoy it—the spectacle more than the event itself. Paula had some technical issues that she wasn't happy about ("Turrnon dee fackeen laights"). Robyn counted her dance steps in a half-hearted attempt to remember the horrible choreography. The waiter took our drink order while people were onstage doing it—as whichever Olsen twin used to say on that garbage-y show, "How rude!"

By the time the Brazilian Lesbians took the stage, I'd managed to relax a little bit. They playfully clawed at each other's ill-fitting leather getups, much to the audible delight (*barf!*) of the gathered pervs. As Gerry Dee says in his strip club joke, you look around at the other people in a place like this and think, "Who are these losers? God. *That* guy was here last Tuesday."

They whipped each other, sorta. They kissed each other, sorta. Then the houselights came up. They needed a volunteer from the crowd.

Joomba-doomba-doomba-doomba, went the '70s bass line. *Clap-clap-clap* went the crowd as the BLs trotted down the front steps of the stage to find their victim. Every other hand in the place shot up. Pick me! *Please!!*

Nothing doing. They made a beeline for me. The least pervy, most clean-cut fish out of water there. I smiled and whispered, "No, thank you."

Joomba-doomba-doomba-doomba.

Clap-clap-clap.

They insisted. Again I declined. Politely.

Joomba-doomba-doomba-doomba.

Boooooo!

The entire crowd started to turn on me because I was bringing the show down. The show I didn't even want to go to in the first place. I looked at Brian, pleading. *Why is this happening? Why don't you go up?* He smiled and shrugged. When in Rome.

Joomba-doomba-doomba-doomba. They pulled me up out of my seat and danced me onstage and the crowd went wild. The show was back on!

The Brazilian Lesbians handed me a whip and bent over. One of them gestured for me to use it on them, but not hard.

I guess I'm a performer at heart, and no matter the stage I want to do a good job. So I mimed whipping them and beamed at the audience like some type of proud lion tamer.

The audience rewarded me with thunderous applause.

I did it again, with a little more vigour. More applause and cheers! I was killing up there, and best of all, not even touching their posteriors with the whip! Showbiz magic!

The rest all happened so quickly. I remember one of them whispering in my ear in very broken English, "I'm going to pull your pants down but not all the way."

"Pardon?"

Joomba-doomba-doomba-doomba. Jiggady-roomba-doomba-boomba.

The other one pulled my khaki shorts down to my ankles—boxer shorts too. Luckily I was bum to the crowd.

They got me down on all fours and proceeded to whip me. Hard. I glanced over my shoulder to make pleading eye contact with Brian, but he couldn't see me through the tears streaming down his cheeks from laughing so hard.

My bottom hurt, as did my pride. But then came the strangest sensation of all. It appeared to be snowing on the stage. Big white flakes falling to the floor below me.

It took me a minute to realize they were my traveller's cheques. Followed by my passport. Birth certificate. And several coins from all the countries we'd visited.

Seasoned travellers had told me before I left for Europe that pick-pocketing was rampant and the best safeguard against the crafty crooks was a money belt. Think of a fanny pack that goes *inside* your shorts. I was wearing one, and evidently the zipper had broken—which is why, after my shorts came down, it was flapping in the breeze and all the contents were now littering the sticky stage. The Brazilian Lesbians just watched as I crawled around half-naked, scurrying to gather my important documents and waddle back to my seat like some kind of humiliated penguin. I muttered something about "keeping the change."

I plopped down in my seat and stared straight ahead, trauma-tized. Brian was covering his mouth in a poor attempt to swallow what were by now big, hearty guffaws.

"Let's get the hell out of here."

"We can't leave now. The next act is starting."

The announcer enthusiastically introduced Maya (not her real name) and the Gorilla (definitely not his real name). "Maya" was a bored-looking Filipino woman, and her partner was somebody in a gorilla suit—Blackman double-dipping, maybe?—with an imitation phallus strapped on.

As Maya danced in a world of her own, the Gorilla simulated self-stimulation. I was still fuming, sitting with my arms crossed in the second row, while Brian chuckled beside me at the absurdity of the spectacle.

I turned to glare at him when I suddenly felt a strange sensation. My face and neck was warm.

Seems as though the gorilla had "finished" on my face. And neck.

I stood up, eyes blurry from whatever it was, and marched with my head held high up the aisle and out the door. Brian followed shortly after, and we didn't talk for the hour-long walk back to our hotel.

Then, in the dark from his bed, I heard . . .

"I can't believe you got spuzzed on by a gorilla."

We laughed 'til the sun came up.

Golfing with Gretz

Taggart

I had a gas hanging out and playing the pro-am at the first Wayne Gretzky and Friends golf tournament at Glen Arbour in the summer of 2000. It was an exhibition where PGA pro Mike Weir would play his best ball against Wayner, Brett Hull and Mario Lemieux. Wayne is a bit of a chop golfer, but Brett Hull is a like a two handicap and Mario is about the same—both are very good golfers. It was pretty much a relaxed three-day party. Put it this way: I don't remember who won, and I don't think anyone cared. It was a big success. There were tons of great fans. I had a terrific time, and I got to meet Gretz, which was pretty cool, because he's Wayne Gretzky.

I walked a couple of holes with the extremely professional Mario Lemieux—who has an amazing golf swing, by the way, easy like

Ernie Els. I ended up going out with Brett Hull and a bunch of other NHLers to the Dome one very late night. Brett is a bahd, for sure— you won't find a much better hang than that guy. Always has a great story, and is so positive. I vaguely remember some classic moments with Tiger Williams by the end of that time at the Dome. What a classic place. Pretty greasy, indeed.

Bahd Ambassador
Bette MacDonald

Cape Breton treasure Bette works with Jono on *Mr. D* but is also known throughout the Maritimes for her yearly Christmas show. She sings, she dances, she blows the roof off place after place with her equally talented husband, Maynard, and her hilarious roster of comedic characters by her side. This show delivers the most laughs per minute of any show you will ever see. Here are Bette's hot tips for Cape Breton.

- The **Doryman Pub & Grill** in Cheticamp is the place to be on any Saturday afternoon. There will be fiddle tunes and square sets.
- The **little lobster shack behind the Island Sunset restaurant** in Belle Cote is a hidden gem.**La Bella Mona Lisa** art gallery in St. Joseph du Moine is a delight
- **Flavor Downtown**, **Flavor on the Water** and **Flavor Nineteen** for the best food in Sydney.
- The **Artisan Trail** for the most unique and beautiful creations by the locals.
- The **Savoy Theatre**, where the White Stripes shot their tenth-anniversary concert DVD.

Fit for the Pizzit

Torrens

During *Street Cents*, Mike Clattenburg and I started making the odd music video. He'd direct and I'd produce. We'd apply for a grant from VideoFact and would always include an element of black-and-white footage in our creative treatment. When we delivered the video, we'd say we shot in black and white, but it didn't really work creatively, so we took it out.

Meanwhile, we were pilfering black-and-white film stock to make our first short film. It was called *Liquor Store* and it starred our muse, Brian Heighton.

Liquor Store won a couple of awards at the Atlantic Film Festival, including a $10,000 prize for best short film. That got us some heat, and the next project we made was a half-hour comedy short for Global called *Nan's Taxi*, about an elderly woman who was the dispatcher for a one-car cab company in a small town. The cab was driven by her two grandsons, played by Daniel Kash and—you guessed it—Brian Heighton.

For a couple of young punks who were used to having a lot of creative freedom, the Global experience was a little suffocating. Lots of script notes, which we weren't used to. Lots of edit notes, which we hated. Ultimately, *Nan's Taxi* went on to win the Gemini Award for best short film in 1997.

Go figure.

As a result of our win, we had some traction at networks and had a show in development at the CBC called *Thanks for Watching*. It was a sketch show, hosted by a news anchor named Gary Canada (played by me!), who would interview the actors from the sketches, not realizing that they were fictitious. I still love the idea today.

But Mike was turned off by the network experience after *Nan's* and had a hankering to do something more lo-fi.

Meanwhile, two guys he went to high school with—Robb Wells and J.P. Tremblay—were living in Charlottetown, where they owned a pizza shop. During the long, cold winters, the boys would videotape themselves and their friend Pat Roach playing silly characters and making each other laugh.

So that summer, Clattenburg made a short film starring them and another friend of his, John Dunsworth.

Then they made another short called *Trailer Park Boys*. And the rest is history.

Mike asked me to play that "eyes all over to one side" character that we always did around the *Street Cents* office, and I was more than happy to.

We were out drinking in Halifax one night, the whole gang of us, and we went to a french fry truck after the bars closed. J.P. turned to me and said, "Pass the ketchup, J-Roc," and the name stuck.

Every network in the country turned the show down except a fledgling cable channel called Showcase. A forward-thinking exec named Laura Michalchyshyn saw the diamond in the rough and ordered six episodes.

Here's some Canadianity for you bahds: we shot the first season of *TPB* in late spring 2000. That winter, two weeks after my triumphant Y2K correspondent gig in Charlottetown, I was in a bad car accident. My femur was broken in multiple places and required surgery. Either because of the drugs or lack of medical knowledge,

I think I grossly underestimated the magnitude of the injury the whole way through.

As an aside, when something like that happens, it's astonishing who surfaces. Pretty sure flowers from the gang at *Air Farce* beat my ambulance to the hospital. Peter Mansbridge even called the nurse's station on my floor to check in on me. Such nice and classy folks.

It was a painful time in a lot of ways, but nothing a few pins and screws couldn't fix. There was only one little problem: after weeks in a wheelchair and months on crutches, I had graduated to a cane, but there was no way I could go without it for the *Trailer Park Boys* shoot. My leg just wasn't strong enough.

Here's the genius of Mike Clattenburg. "No problem," he said. "We'll just rock it for the character."

And the crazy thing is, it worked. If you watch season 1, J-Roc had a part gangsta, part-Dream Warrior vibe.

That's what I always say about Clattenburg. He just sees things that others don't. Like the way Gretzky somehow knew where the puck was *going*, we could do a few takes of a scene and it would be funny—really funny—and then Mike would suggest doing it again, but giving Randy a bag of BBQ chips, and suddenly it was off-the-charts hilarious. It's quite a gift. As producer Mike Volpe says, it's like a fairy dust that he sprinkles over top of things to make them next-level.

Those early *Trailer Park Boys* seasons were really special. What we lacked in resources we more than made up for in spirit. My stomach hurt from laughing all day between takes, and my inner cheeks were permanently scarred from biting them to try not to laugh during.

We moved from park to park, season to season. When we were shooting in real parks, I think it sounded like a novelty at first to have a TV show shoot in your midst. The reality is, by the end of the season, Ricky yelling "I'm gonna get drunk and eat chicken fingers" into a megaphone twenty takes in a row kind of loses its charm.

Much has been written about the popularity of the show, but I think it comes down to three things:

1. Nobody in Sunnyvale is feeling sorry for themselves, even though they're living lives that some would deem subpar. All Ricky wants is to start growing great dope so he can provide for his family. All Bubbles wants is food for his kitties. These are simple, relatable goals.

2. Watching these guys makes you feel a bit better about your own life.

3. Like any family, when external forces conspire against them, they put aside their differences and band together. No one calls Bubbles a disparaging R-word. No one judges Randy and Lahey's relationship. No one questions that J-Roc isn't black. It just is. What a nice message. Clattenburg always said, "When you take away the guns, dope and swearing, it's a show about family."

When the first season dropped, I thought the rap community might misinterpret J-Roc as making fun of them, but I couldn't have been more wrong. I got lots of nice notes and props from rappers, saying thank God someone's finally making fun of those whack MCs rolling around in Chevettes on twenty-inch spinners from Canadian Tire.

Meanwhile, most of the real J-Roc dudes I met responded with some version of "Yo, thanks for repping us on TV, dawg!"

Unbelievable. I somehow landed in the valley between both camps on that one. Bullet dodged!

The things that J-Roc has are overconfidence and underperformance. That's my favourite comic wheelhouse. On paper, J-Roc and Robert Cheeley from *Mr. D* are very different characters, but upon closer examination, their egos are both writing cheques that their ability can't cash.

Trailer Park Boys, on the other hand, wasn't so well received. *Globe and Mail* critic John Doyle destroyed it in his first review. He didn't get it, didn't want it, didn't understand. To his credit, a year later he published another column admitting that he'd completely missed the charm and allure of the show and was, from that moment on, a huge fan.

It aired on BBC America—bleeped. Imagine trying to understand the plot of a *TPB* episode with the swear words censored.

But slowly, surely, through word of mouth and with the aforementioned help of bands and teams on buses, it started to become part of the public landscape.

TPB really is the cockroach of Canadian comedy, in that it just won't die. I don't mean for that to sound like I'm wishing it would—not at all. It's just astonishing to me that it keeps finding new life, with new age groups, in new corners of the world. Inconceivable, really, that some teenage boys in Denmark would find it funny. But quite a trip that they do.

Mafk

Torrens

I'm proud to say that "mafk" has made it into the urban dictionary, courtesy of J-Roc. Technically it's short for "motherf*cker," but the word has taken on its own meaning to me. I see it as kind of synonymous with "nerd." It's a term of endearment, certainly.

It was also a pretty creative way to get around the CRTC rules and regulations dealing with swearing on TV. Technically, "mafk" isn't a word, so there's no legal reason it can't be said. Unlike its properly spelled root word.

One of the things I like to do on social media is give a shout-out to the mafk, the guy doing/wearing something that everyone has seen but maybe no one's pointed out before. For some reason, the plural is "mafsks."

Let's look at some examples:

- Shout-out to the mafk walking through the airport wearing a neck pillow.
- Shout-out to those bald-headed mafsks with beards.
- Shout-out to the mafk pre-pounding two Ferrero Rochers while waiting in line to pay for them at Shoppers.
- Shout-out to the mafk swerving into my lane trying to dip a McNugget.
- Shout-out to the mafk trying to look hard on a flip phone.
- Shout-out to the fifty-five-year-old mafk in a Thing 2 hoodie. I see you, dawg.

- Shout-out to the mafk filling a jerry can with sunglasses on his face *and* on top of his head.
- Shout-out to the mafk with the super-tanned left arm from dangling it out the truck window all summer.
- Shout-out to the mafk who posts up in the friend zone, just waiting to pounce as soon as she becomes single again.
- Shout-out to the spider-legged mafk in school with creases on his jeans from where his mom let down the hem every few months.
- Shout-out to the mafk still tossing out *Borat* quotes.
- Shout-out to the mafsks who always try to anticipate the end of your sentence and say it along with you.
- Shout-out to the mafsks who are super-proud to tell you they don't own a TV.
- Shout-out to the mafsks who clap when the plane lands.
- Shout-out to the mafk who rolled into the duty-free just to spray himself with cologne and then leave.

Blank-Lookin' Mafk is another classic game, and one of the things that Jeremy and I bonded over in the first place. You just have to describe someone in a photograph with an obscure reference. Could be a celebrity or one of your bahds.

We played Blank-Lookin' Mafk on the podcast, and others joined in right away. Turbo-bahd Tyler Stewart from Barenaked Ladies called Ed Robertson a "News Anchor at Home on a Sunday–Lookin' Mafk." I called Tyler a "Built a BBQ Out of an Old Oil Barrel for the Camp–Lookin' Mafk." It's easy and fun!

Here's a list of a few famous Canadians you can try, with our suggestions:

- **Mike Myers:** Regional Manager at Staples–Lookin' Mafk

- **Jim Cuddy from Blue Rodeo:** Just Started Dating Your Mom, but You're Actually Cool with It–Lookin' Mafk

- **P.K. Subban:** Funniest Guy Behind the Desk at the Local Y–Lookin' Mafk

- **Nelly Furtado:** Wishes There Was Something She Could Do to Help but Her Hands Are Tied Customer Service Rep–Lookin' Mafk.

This mafk talk inspired a game called Who Dis Canadian Mafk? in which the third clue was always "I'm a _____–Lookin' Mafk." See how you do:

Who Dis Canadian Mafk?

1. I am a stoner from BC.
   I have the most annoying laugh since Eddie Murphy.
   I'm a Works at the Genius Bar–Lookin' Mafk.

2. I am an Ottawa native.
   I am an actor and a musician.
   I'm a Works at a Rental Car Counter–Lookin' Mafk.

3. I have a beard.
   I drive a motorcycle.

I'm a Guy Your Sister Met on Tinder and Brought Home for Thanksgiving Dinner–Lookin' Mafk.

4. I am an indie movie actor.

I was in *Juno*.

I'm a Works at Radio Shack–Lookin' Mafk.

5. I am a piano tinkler from Vancouver Island.

Nothing turns me on more than the sound of my own voice.

I'm a David Cronenberg–Lookin' Mafk.

6. I am a TSN on-air personality.

I am of Italian descent.

I am a Your Dad's Friend Who's Going Through a Rough Time–Lookin' Mafk.

7. I am a button-pushing beat music guy from Ontario.

I wear a huge mask while I perform, but paint my Lambo so people know it's me rollin' by.

I'm a Make It Quick, Barista–Lookin' Mafk.

8. I am a singer.

I am Québécoise.

I am a Marsha from the Office Who Brings Stinky Lunches–Lookin' Mafk.

9. I was born in 1980 in London, Ontario.

My mom's name was Donna.

I'm a Cobbler at Black Creek Pioneer Village–Lookin' Mafk.

10. I have a famous last name.

    I just got a big new job.

    I'm an I'd Be Happy to Tutor Your Girlfriend—Really, It's No Problem–Lookin' Mafk.

11. I live in Ottawa now.

    I'm an athlete who's been known to crush the odd dart.

    I'm a One More Strike and You're Out HR Nightmare Who Works Nights at the Warehouse His Dad Owns–Lookin' Mafk.

    Bonus Hint: I'm a Could Easily Have Been Cast as the Older Brother on *The Wonder Years*–Lookin' Mafk.

12. I was born in Vancouver in 1976.

    I did some *National Lampoon* movies.

    I'm an I'm Taking Your Idea, I Don't Care–Lookin' Mafk.

13. I am a singer with a stage name.

    I am from a small town in Northern Ontario.

    I'm a Volunteers at the SPCA Where I Work Have Gone Through the Roof Since I Started Here–Lookin' Mafk.

14. I was born in Kingston, Ontario.

    I like to party, and the world pretty much knows it.

    I'm a Go Ahead, Roll Another One at the Local Bowling Alley–Lookin' Mafk.

15. I was born in Kapuskasing, Ontario, in 1954.

    I've directed some of the biggest movies of all time.

I'm a What's with the Plastic Forks, Knives and Straws?–Lookin' Mafk.

16. I am a news broadcaster.

I am recently retired.

I'm a Sits on the Board of the Toronto Symphony *and* the Art Gallery of Ontario–Lookin' Mafk.

1. Seth Rogen; 2. Tom Green; 3. Keanu Reeves; 4. Michael Cera; 5. David Foster; 6. Gino Reda; 7. Deadmau5; 8. Céline Dion; 9. Ryan Gosling; 10. Justin Trudeau; 11. Dion Phaneuf; 12. Ryan Reynolds; 13. Shania Twain; 14. Dan Aykroyd; 15. James Cameron; 16. Lloyd Robertson.

Nova Scotia Gotta Do's

GO BIRLIN' to Sugar Moon Farm. Pancakes and hikes. Sausages and syrup. Lazy Sunday morning spot in the middle of the province.

DEMOLISH breakfast at Annie's Place Cafe in Halifax. Food is delicious, but Annie's company makes it not to be missed.

TAKE A RIP down to Kingsburg Beach, outside Lunenburg. Less populated than some other South Shore hotspots. Exactly the reason it's worth the trip off the beaten path.

HOP on the Dartmouth ferry. A great and cost-effective way to see Halifax from the water. Sit on the open-air deck with a coffee and . . .

OBLITERATE a chocolate croissant at Two If by Sea. They're heavier than doorstops. TIBS's watchword for baked goods is simple: *butter*.

CRUSH the lobster-encrusted haddock at Chives. Fresh homemade biscuits served before your meal too.

POP down to Pictou Lodge. Rustic spot to spend the night if you're into bonfires and the person you're with.

INHALE the haddock at Bing's Eatery in Maitland. Delicious slow food that'll help warm you up after whitewater rafting on the Bay of Fundy, home to the world's largest tides. Bing's has delicious summer cocktails too, like rosemary vodka lemonade.

SCOPE some whales at Brier Island. If whale watching is your bag, do it here. Scientific research vessels that get just close enough to give you a thrill, but stay just far enough away so as not to disrupt nature's plan.

CRUISE the Cabot Trail in the fall. Leaves are bananas. Scenery is nuts. Hospitality is so friendly, it's almost unsettling.

WHIP into Bistro 22 in the T-Dot (Truro). Chef Dennis is a certified bahd (look for the BAHD sticker on his cooler!), and his biscuits are tight as a cobra's taint.

Quebec: Expos and Sex Shows

Bahd Bands

Leonard Cohen

Oscar Peterson

Mitsou

Corey Hart

Luba

Arcade Fire

Men Without Hats

Wolf Parade

Stars

The Box

Simple Plan

Five Notable Bahds

Chuck Hughes. With tats that read *lobster* and *bacon* on his forearms, Chuck is a manic monster in the kitchen, whipping up unreal meals from whatever they're selling at the market that day. I mean, *lobster poutine.*

Jacob Tierney. Director of *The Trotsky* and one of the best directors Torrens has ever worked with. Fast and funny. Also directs/co-writes/acts in *Letterkenny Problems,* which cements his status as bahd of all bahds.

Jay Baruchel. Is there anyone Montrealier than this? Even though he was born in Ottawa. Wrote *Goon*. Wrote and directed *Goon 2*. Heavy Canadianity.

Jessica Paré. *Mad Men*. Nomesayin'?

Russell Martin. This Mixologist in a Bowtie with Suspenders–Lookin' Mafk is the catcher for the Toronto Blue Jays. Cultured, chippy and has weathered some storms. Cool qualities.

Or as We Say in the Maritimes, "Kwee-beck"

Torrens

Quebec is a wild place, man. One of the most interesting things about it is that it has its own built-in star system in a way that the rest of Canada doesn't. A hit TV show in Quebec routinely gets a million viewers a week. You can say that about very few shows in English Canada—and most of them are Canadian versions of US formats.

As worldly as Montreal and Quebec City are, with the *cinq-à-sept* postwork cocktail culture and *tam-tam-sur-la-montagne* drum sessions, rural Quebec is its own deal too. Buttered pizza crust and roadside strip joints.

The Flying Ham Sandwich

Taggart

My first time in Quebec.

Baseball has been a passion of mine since I was four. I loved to play it. I also loved all the different things you needed to know when playing it. My dad really worked hard to make me understand the importance of practice. He said, "You should hit like Ted Williams," so that meant swinging the bat five hundred times a day. He said, "You should pitch like Sandy Koufax," which meant throwing fifty strikes. He said, "You should field like Pee Wee Reese," so that meant successfully fielding dozens of batted balls. He always took practice so seriously. All in, all the time.

I somehow dug it too. I could feel my game get better, and it made baseball much more fun because I could compete. I wanted to affect the game at that point. I'd hit with a broomstick and he'd throw tiny rocks. He figured if I could get used to hitting that way, then hitting the ball with a bat would be a snap.

All that crazy practice is what led to my drumming ability. The understanding of refining and working on all the little things. I was a decent pitcher and player only because I practised my ass off. I got hits because I expected them and struck guys out because I felt I deserved to succeed more than the batter.

I played rep ball from the age of eight on and enjoyed the routine of weekday practising and travel that happened every weekend. Sometimes I'd go away for longer periods of time, like when I was around eleven and had a tournament in Trois-Rivières, where I stayed with one of the local team's families. It was a trip! I took

French in school every year but couldn't understand a word, and they didn't know much English, so we didn't talk much. I hung out with the kid my age, and we did our best to communicate. They were very nice and took great care of me.

We played on the Commodore 64, and I would watch the entire family eat cheese curds. They would have a meal, then rip open a bag of cheese curds and crush it in minutes. I'd never had them before, and to be honest, I was never much of a cheese kid—plus the squeakiness when you bite into a cheese curd kind of turned me off after a couple. They would just rip that bag open and they'd get right into it after lunch and dinner like a ritual.

The baseball was fantastic, and they had live francophone announcers in the little *stade de baseball*, bringing each batter to the plate with classic local flair. It really added to the vibe of the game. So cool to see how big baseball was in Quebec. Big crowds and teams from all over. People sometimes forget the history of baseball in Canada. It's so deep! We get so horny about hockey that baseball exists in its shadow.

My parents came for the end of the week to see a couple of games and to drive me home, and my dad almost killed himself on one of those long, swingy chain-link fences. He did that thing when you step over the chain-link mesh, but then trip on it, and then fall into it and go ass over teakettle to the ground. He wrenched his back badly, and that ten-hour drive home didn't help it. Poor Ronnie.

When I was fifteen and living in the Finch and Weston Road area of Toronto, Dad and I would practise behind this church near the Humber River. I'd pitch, swing the bat and hit little rocks into the creek. One afternoon we were walking back to our apartment after a long, solid shift, when we heard these kids screaming and hanging out of the windows of a greasy black van ripping down Weston Road towards us. Just as they passed us, I saw an object launch from the hand of the moron in the shotgun seat.

I saw the sun reflect off it, so I was worried that it might be glass. It whistled directly into my dad's right eye and face. They must have been going eighty kilometres an hour, so whatever the object was, it was moving. It smashed into Dad's face and exploded everywhere. Dad dropped his glove and bat and recoiled from the impact, his arms stretched out wide from shock. Then he started screaming and rubbing his eyes.

"Fucking mustard! It's fucking mustard! It's burning my eyes! *Who throws a fucking ham sandwich?! Fucking warmongers, that's who!*" Yes, they threw a ham sandwich at us, and all its contents were Vitamixed from the impact, directly into my dad's right eye socket. He probably took in some calories, that's how much of it made it into his eye. Fucking punks.

I recognized them from the metal shop class at Emery Collegiate. My brother Jetsun was just getting home in his VW Rabbit when the sandwich hit the fan. Dad raged his way up to him. Ronnie wanted to chase after these guys, with his eye all mustardy. He screamed about how he was going to get them as he ripped out the driveway and down Weston Road in a rage. We could hear him driving furiously around the neighbourhood as I explained the situation to Jet. Dad never found them, despite ripping around for a good thirty minutes. He cooled off and went in the house to clean up. Those losers who threw the sandwich were always doing dumb shit like that. On the road to dead or in jail.

Naked Ambition

Torrens

 When I was eighteen, I was working on *Street Cents*. We'd rehearse in Halifax on Sundays and shoot in studio on Monday and Tuesday. Often on Wednesday, I'd hit the road to various parts of the country to shoot stories for that week's episode.

I loved being on the road. Going out with blank tapes and returning with raw TV was so exciting to me. Staying in hotels and sitting in restaurants by myself, in places I'd never been. It felt so romantic somehow.

Always in the back of my mind was that my experience was so unlike what most people my age were doing. All my friends were making bad decisions and doing frosh week activities while I was at a helmet factory shooting a What's Your Beef? segment for *Street Cents*.

I wouldn't trade it for anything, but every now and then I'd think maybe I should do some things that were more age-appropriate.

It's the same with friends. Every now and then I think, "Why don't I have a group of close friends that I hang out with?" So I'll spend a month or two trying to get together with folks, and then I remember—I don't like that. I'm very social and enjoy being around new people all the time, but I don't like to commit.

So one snowy night in December when I was eighteen, I was killing time in my room and decided I should go to a strip club. By myself. Because that's what young men do.

There weren't many of us, seeing as it was probably seven o'clock.

I sat nervously nursing my Bailey's and milk when a young woman approached me. This would never happen in any other environment. She sat down and asked what I was doing in town. I didn't want to blow my CBC kids show cover, so I mumbled something about a family reunion.

She asked if I wanted her to dance for me. I gulped and said yes.

She produced a milk crate–like object and stood up on it right in front of me, in an almost empty room. She started to disrobe and I. Did. Not. Break. Eye. Contact. It seemed rude to look.

The song finished and she asked if I wanted her to dance to another song. I said, "Sure, but can I ask you something first?"

She shrugged and nodded in the neon light.

"Does your dad know you do this?"

Buzzkill, right? She sat down beside me and I thought, "Here's my shot. I'll never get this chance again." I went into full Linden MacIntyre *Fifth Estate* mode:

"Do you practise?"

"How many outfits do you own?"

"Does the club pay for them?"

"What do you think about while you're dancing?"

"Has doing this desensitized you when it comes to intimacy?"

"Has a classmate or relative ever walked in while you're onstage?"

"Do you ever get cold?"

"Are you using your real name?"

"Can you call in sick?"

"Have you ever dated a customer?"

I was fascinated. Turns out she was not using her real name. Can you even believe that?

Not surprisingly, she confessed that my line of questioning left her feeling not much like dancing anymore and she asked if I wanted to grab a bite somewhere and talk.

Sure, I said. What else was I doing?

So she talked to her boss and asked if she could leave.

Canadianity Strip Club Playlist

When these tracks were recorded, the artists may not have known that they were destined to be disrobed to by a Canadian stripper with a name like Louise Lake or Titsou.

"Rockstar" (Nickelback)

"Buzz" (Haywire)

"Insensitive" (Jann Arden)

"Try" (Blue Rodeo)

"Heaven" (Bryan Adams)

"What Does It Take" (Honeymoon Suite)

"Dream Come True" (Frozen Ghost)

"Eurasian Eyes" (Corey Hart)

"Dangerous" (Kardinal Offishall)

"Wild Horses" (Gino Vannelli)

"Perfect" (Simple Plan)

We went to an all-night diner and talked all night. She told me that what she really wanted to do was be a flight attendant because she loved to travel. The problem was, the money was just too good at Super Sexe (okay, guys, *d'accord les guys!*). I listened and encouraged her to chase her dreams.

In the morning, she dropped me off at my hotel and kissed me on the cheek. It was like a weird, reverse date that started naked and ended fully clothed.

I keep waiting to get on a flight and see her because, to optimistic me, that's how things work.

Honeymoon

I love Quebec City. It's a great place that's so close for me in Toronto that my wife, Lisa, and I had our honeymoon there. We stayed at the Auberge Saint-Antoine, an incredible five-star spot in the old part of the city, surrounded by art galleries and cafés. It's like you just got off an eight-hour flight to Europe.

I have so much respect for the province of Quebec. The people really understand the importance of culture and maintaining their own history. From musicians to painters to actors, you can be successful and never have to leave the province. I don't know why other places in Canada are in such a hurry to catch up with American culture. From pop-culture icons to fast food, so many cities are blurring into a standard Western existence. Not so in Quebec. André-Philippe Gagnon could fill theatres for a month there, and Corey Hart could sell out arenas for shits and giggles. The Quebec people lead the country in terms of loving their own icons.

Growing up in Ontario, it was the complete opposite. We can't wait to move on to the next big thing in Ontario. It's a total bummer.

I don't understand why we tire so quickly of our own, or like something more because it's American or whatever. Some people even find it embarrassing that Quebec and some parts of the East Coast embrace their roots and their popular artists. This is a shame and completely ignorant. I wish the people who share that greener-grass mentality would get on a Monsanto rocket and move to Mars.

When I started with OLP, we did small tours in Quebec. Places like Sherbrooke, Trois-Rivières, Jonquière and Drummondville were the places we cut our teeth and grew a following. In fact, MusiquePlus was the first network to really push us. Our first actual show was in Montreal at a bar called Backstreet. We were opening for the Tea Party on a small tour that was arranged by a mutual friend and upstart promoter named D.J. Williams, who went to Ridley College in St. Catharines with Duncan and Raine.

That show we played at Backstreet had to be the absolute worst show ever by any band. Somewhere in the middle of playing our song "Naveed," we went right off the rails. Like, off-the-cliff-and-down-the-mountain style. Nobody had a clue where we were, and we couldn't get it back. We had to stop playing. So bad. We were so embarrassed that we got off the stage. Fucking classic example of live and learn, bahds. It was impossible to do any worse, so the next show was great, just because we made it through the entire set.

The Bifteck on Boulevard St-Laurent is a great place to get banged up. Great vibe of old-school Montreal, and there's always a bahd from a local great band hanging there. Poutine anywhere is always a good move after crushing a late-night round with your bahds.

Jared Keeso

Jared Keeso is one of those rare actors who can pull off dramatic and comedic roles with exacting proficiency. We first noticed him in the lead role of Don Cherry in the CBC mini-series *Keep Your Head Up, Kid: The Don Cherry Story* and *Wrath of Grapes: The Don Cherry Story II*.

The Listowel, Ontario, native co-created and stars in *Letterkenny Problems*, one of the funniest shows in Canadian comedy history. It tells the story of three groups coexisting in a small town: the hicks, the skids and the jocks. From the moment it arrived on the internet as a series of shorts, fans (including us) were rabid for it. It stands up as a half-hour hick-com in a big way.

But it was the exceptional cop series *19-2*, which airs on Bravo, that took Jared to Montreal, which he now calls home.

Here are just a few places he'd suggest you **CRUSH** a pint:

- **Pub St-Paul in Old Montreal.** Building went up in the late 1800s. Great spot. They have cover bands every Friday and Saturday night.
- **Taverne St-Sacrement in the Plateau.** Trendy Montreal rocker bar. Small stage in a far corner of the room. This place is always packed.
- **Les Torchés in the Plateau.** Another favourite, always packed too.

Okay, Guys, D'Accord les Guys

Torrens

Somehow on *TnT* we started talking like Quebec roadside strip club DJs. If you've ever driven through Rivière-du-Loup, you've seen this kind of place. It's a motel. It's a grocery store. And—if you can believe the sign—it's a destination for "XXX Danseuse Nues" too.

We decided our fictitious club would be in Sherbrooke, and Jeremy came up with the name Popular Girl.

There are a few things that struck us funny about this. Who are the people that would end up working there as bouncers and DJs? Like, the minor leagues of adult entertainment. Couldn't even make it on Rue Ste-Catherine in Montreal, the Broadway of barenakedness.

Two, the song choices. Taggart always picks strange tempos like "Conga" by Miami Sound Machine. How on earth could you peel off the gear to that track?

Then there are the theme nights, like "Sexpos de Montreal" night with feature dancer Hairy Carter.

The real danger of Popular Girl is in the rowdiness of the imaginary patrons and their desire to throw *"les loonies et puit les twonies"* at the dancers. Understandably, this results in real friction between the performers and the crowd.

We love Popular Girl so much, we briefly entertained the notion of trying to open one. But then we felt gross about ourselves.

Ay Ma! Joe Took My Brio!

Torrens

For some reason we also started doing a sketch on the pod called "The Vannelli Brothers." Born out of the idea of Gino and his brother Joe as kids growing up in Montreal, tormenting their *maaaaaa* from the basement.

The fraternal tension was largely rooted in which one had stolen the other one's Brio. Our version of the Vannellis somehow imagines Gino and Joe still living at home long after Gino has had huge hits on the radio. This is an animated series just waiting to happen.

Meanwhile, two Vannelli games were born out of this concept. Play for yourself and see how you do!

Vannelli or Vannelli's?

The first game is Vannelli or Vannelli's, where we take turns reading a review and the other guy has to guess whether it's from a review of a Gino concert or of the food court staple Mrs. Vannelli's.

1. "I was sweaty 'cause it was hot but the taste was amazing here. What a night!"

2. "The guy should smile more."

3. "It was really good and definitely helped keep my hangover at bay—which is enough to keep me coming back."

4. "Not too long of a line!"

5. "I got my gut busted. Blown away again!"

6. "Filled with skill and passion."

7. "You may even get free demonstrations of people jamming to music to keep all the crazy line moving and people in high spirits. Don't worry, they got a dude at the door late those evenings to make sure those folks that think they're about to cut the line, don't."

8. "It was a good mix!"

9. "I wish I didn't have lage or I woulda had a better time here."

10. "Slightly generic."

11. "What power and flavour. I can't get enough of these guys. Always a family favourite."

12. "A real gem."

13. "I think they'll be in big business for a long time to come."

14. "Surprisingly, it was not overdone!"

15. "Not too expensive."

Vannelli: 1, 6, 8, 13 and 14. Vannelli's: 2, 3, 4, 5, 7, 9, 10, 11, 12 and 15.

Rio or Brio?

The original inspired our second Vannelli game: Rio or Brio. During the 2016 Summer Olympics in Rio de Janeiro, there were lots of complaints about the venues, the safety and the hospitality to visiting athletes. Our favourite story was of a canoeist reportedly hitting a partially submerged *couch* in the water during time trials. See if you can guess whether the following reviews are of Rio or Brio:

1. "Both speak to living with vigor and vivacity, to being spirited and alive and to exhibiting one's life force."
2. "It's excellent but sadly underrated."
3. "I've seen that names somewhere so next time I see it, I'll be looking for it."
4. "My eyes are stinging."
5. "There's actual shit in the water."
6. "I haven't tried it but I'd like to someday."
7. "It isn't great but it isn't bad either."
8. "To be honest, I almost vomited."
9. "There's so much garbage in it."
10. "Even now, I'm still amazed I've got this thing in my hand."
11. "Best water in the central zone."

Rio: 4, 5, 7, 8, 9 and 10. Brio: 1, 2, 3, 6 and 11.

Quebec Gotta Do's

HANG in Old Quebec, with its galleries, restaurants and historic forti-fied walls.

RIP the Laurentides on a bike.

CRUSH the sights at Montmorency Falls Park or Forillon National Park.

FORAGE for festivals like Jazz Fest, Just for Laughs or Osheaga in Montreal.

DESTROY poutine at Lafayette Hot Dog 1870 in Montreal.

JAM some culture at the Canadian Museum of History in Gatineau.

MUSH a dog team in the Chaudière-Appalaches region.

SHIVER YOUR TIMBERS with a stay at the Hôtel de Glace (the only ice hotel in North America).

PEEP birds on Bonaventure Island. Sit in the bush with binoculars with-out worrying about looking pervy, 'cuz everyone else is too.

DEMOLISH a slice at Sapori Di Napoli in Montreal.

Manitobahds

Bahd Bands

The Guess Who

Burton Cummings

Randy Bachman

Crash Test Dummies

Neil Young

The Watchmen

The Weakerthans

The Wailin' Jennys

Susan Aglukark

Terry Jacks

Five Notable Bahds

Anna Paquin. *True Blood. X-Men. The Squid and the Whale.* But first seen in *The Piano,* for which she won an Oscar at age eleven.

Donnelly Rhodes. Journeyman Canadian actor. The dad on *Danger Bay!*

Jonathan Toews. Puck bahd. Arguably the second-best all-around player in the NHL after Sid. Won just about every accolade possible, from medals to Cups.

Monte Halperin. Better known as Monty Hall, the host of *Let's Make a Deal.*

Nia Vardalos. *My Big Fat Greek Wedding* put her on the worldwide map.

The Drive to Winnipeg

Taggart

It's a fuck of a long drive from Toronto to Winnipeg. There is no better word in the English language than "fuck" to measure the feeling of that goddamned length of a drive. It breaks you down when you sit and wait for Ontario to end. The first "fuck" hits you in Sudbury. That's when you get a good four-hour punch in the gut that leaves you with the pain of knowing you haven't even started getting out of Ontario yet and the understanding that this is gonna be a while. Fuck me.

The straight shot to Winni is a backbreaker. You don't appreciate it the first time. I sat in the back of our tour van, spending my time sleeping or chatting. You've told your life story by Sault Ste. Marie, and you're arguing by Marathon. It never stops. It's like George Chuvalo in his prime. You aren't going to beat it with ease. It's going to take you to your inner limit and test your relationship with everyone in the vehicle.

Fuck! You're only in Nipigon! It's been fourteen hours and you've still got a couple of seasons of *The Beachcombers* to go, bahd! Thun-der Bay for a piss and you think you're almost there, and then you make the mistake of asking how much farther it is. Another ten hours? Fuck. You start questioning the maps at this point, looking at them to explain to you this bullshit madness of how big Ontario is. By the time you hit Dryden you are numb, thinking all of Canada is a joke you weren't in on and that Ontario is the only province. By the time you hit Kenora, you would bet money on Ontario never ending.

Then the winding and rolling road starts to straighten . . . and you're in Manitoba! The sense of accomplishment is kind of hollow, but it feels like you've been saved from a deserted island and you're gonna make it to see another day.

The first time I was in Winnipeg, it was for a show where OLP opened for I Mother Earth at the Zoo in Osborne Village. We stayed at the hotel attached to it. What a place. The absolute winner of the Canadianity Greasies. Needles under the beds, hookers knocking on your door all night, arguments and banged-up people everywhere. This was the good stuff. Reality, strong and indiscriminate. The soap in the bathroom would shatter like glass if dropped. That's class.

The music venue was also pretty hardcore. Three huge, bald bouncers and a little bald guy who was clearly trying to be accepted. I say this because he was the subject of the kind of bullying I've never seen since. For example, two of the big bouncers would hold the little guy against the pool table, while the third would run from across the room and jump onto him. This happened several times. Upon load-in in the alley, I saw what looked like a large spine sitting in the corner. I'm not sure if it was animal. What a place!

The place was absolutely jammed. It was my first real taste of Winnipeg music fans. They were going apeshit—it was incredible. There was a rope across the front of the stage instead of the modern barricades. They were stage diving, moshing and singing along. The mad, burling bouncers were totally handling them too, catching flying bodies like rag dolls and putting them down with ease. It was so fresh and aggressive to me, a controlled chaos. I loved it.

It was such a great energy that I became a huge fan of Winnipeg. That ridiculously long drive was worth it. I'd spent all my youth in southern Ontario. Seeing all the character in Winnipeg, I really needed that understanding and perspective. So friendly and also so real. It's great to see how much it's grown since. Having the Jets back is nice too. I always enjoy my time there.

Two days after that wicked show at the Zoo, I was in Brandon, another classic spot. I can't remember much about that day other than it was April 7—my birthday. I was sitting in the mini–school bus/tour van that we'd bought after *Naveed* was released. It was a full-blown *A-Team*-style mini-RV. Plenty of benches that folded flat and a cargo area for our gear, secured by a steel wall that Mike Turner welded quite nicely. It had an army barracks vibe. Hence the *A-Team* reference.

I was sitting in the van and waiting to drive to Regina when I heard the news that Kurt Cobain had been found dead in his house, and he had died by suicide. It was the shittiest news. It was really jarring. Nirvana was such a perfect blend of actual punk feeling and integrity, married with an understanding of pop songs. Kurt had one of the strongest voices of his generation, but he kind of got lost on his path somewhere. That drive to Regina was pretty quiet. Perfect long, straight drive to collect your thoughts.

Bahd Ambassadors
Jay Onrait and Brittney Thomas-Ljungberg

We asked TSN anchor and turbo-bahd Jay Onrait to be a Bahd Ambassador. Not only did he deliver what he knew (coming up in Saskatchewan), but he also subcontracted Winnipeg to his friend Brittney. Here are her solid Winnipeg tips!

The thing about Winnipeg is that we hole up for several months of the year. Everyone seems to have a bunch of side projects or cool things going on, so most places have multiple uses or an equally cool sister project.

- **Clementine.** Beautiful breakfasts, cocktails, juices and coffee in the basement of a heritage building in the Exchange District.
- **Forth.** A multi-floor establishment. On the first floor is a coffee roaster and café that makes great food and gorgeous coffees. Below is a dark, candlelit cocktail bar that lets you sabre your own champagne bottles, as well as an art gallery. In the nicer months, you can head upstairs to the rooftop for parties.
- **Vera.** Classic pizzas done right. On Mondays there's a $1 corkage fee and you'll see a lot of industry regulars around. In summertime they have a cute patio to enjoy. Did I mention how much we love patios? Short summers mean we really wanna take it all in.
- **Bar Italia.** Best patio in the entire city. During the day you can make pals with old Italian men. At night it's got a nice, friendly dive bar feeling, with pinball and VLTs. If you aren't avoiding your ex, you're there to go home with your next.
- **The Handsome Daughter.** This place is 80 percent bar and 20 percent restaurant. The food is great here at night, and they do *the best* eggs benny on the weekends. However, the Handsome Daughter is mostly a venue for music shows, various trivia nights and karaoke. Staff have a wonderfully dark sense of humour.
- **Sous Sol.** Weird little French restaurant in a basement, staffed by a few lovable weirdos. Menu is ever-changing, cocktail program is amazing and there are always some inside jokes hidden on the menu. Only open on the weekends, and they love doing chef's table.
- **Deer + Almond.** Inventive food done by a group of inventive

people. Wine, great cocktails and a few beers. The art and plates are even thoughtfully unique.

- **Máquè.** This is one of Scott Bagshaw's restaurants. Basically, anything he does is worth checking out. This one is Asian, with plates for sharing, other than their amazing steamed buns. No cocktails here, though. Just wine, beer and perhaps some whisky. If you're waiting for a table, head to nearby Close Company, a tiny cocktail bar, in the meantime.

Playing in the 'Peg

Torrens

That's the thing about Manitoba: people show up.

It's a special place. Any band or standup comic will tell you there are no better audiences than Manitoba audiences. Manito-bahds buy their tickets early and stay late. For whatever reason, easily two-thirds of the viewer letters to *Street Cents* were from The Pas, Manitoba.

The first time I discovered this firsthand was when we were doing some *Jonovision* episodes on location at the Forks in Winnipeg and hundreds of kids showed up. That was also the first time I tried an authentic pierogi. Whoa. Both events left me feeling overwhelmed and delighted and with a lump in my throat.

We did a "Jonopalooza" episode with headliners Jet Set Satellite and a bunch of local kid bands. There was one in particular called the Rock Band, and I still listen to their CD all the time. I loved that we were able to give these young bands national exposure on TV. What a thrill that must've been for them.

We also did a "Matchmaker 2000" ep. It's a great concept. Three teenaged boys were asked a series of *Newlywed Game*–style questions by a teenaged girl and her dad. Then the girl and the dad voted for which guy was the best fit. So the girl asked questions like "If you were an animal, which animal would you be?" The dad asked questions more like "Gimme one reason I shouldn't kick your a**?" If they got a match, the pair went out on a date paid for by us. Good, clean fun. And funny.

Jonovision was always a wrestling match between the comedy show for teenagers that we wanted to make and the kids-talk-about-the-issues show that the CBC wanted. So it ended up being both. Sometimes it was a sketch show, sometimes a chat show. That dichotomy is also what made it fun to watch, because you never knew on any given day what the show might be.

It was a blast in our fifth and final season to take it on the road, and I'll never forget the Winnipeg stop. When you shoot something in a studio, you kind of forget that it goes out into the world until you venture out and meet people firsthand who know every sketch and remember things you don't. It's the same with *TnT*.

Another time, I was in Manitoba with John Dunsworth and Pat Roach, better known as Lahey and Randy from *Trailer Park Boys*. We played the Burton Cummings Theatre to a packed house of Sunnyvale fans, and then the same the next night in Brandon.

John Dunsworth is a fascinating creature. Razor sharp and eccentric. Mischievous and confident. He built a rock wall to shelter his home from the sea by collecting boulders one at a time from ditches along the highway on his nightly drives home from the set. Neither he nor his mind ever stop. One of my proudest achievements in life is beating him at Scrabble. Once. He's in the 600-to-700-points-a-game range.

An actor for over forty years, John understands and appreciates more than anyone what a rare lightning-in-a-bottle quality *Trailer Park Boys* has. He'll instantly go into character for anyone who asks—anywhere, anytime. At a traffic light, in a restaurant, at a gas station. He also secretly loves it when people tell him to "*F*ck off, Lahey!*"

John has taught me so many great lessons about acting. He is so fearless and committed in the role of Lahey, and he does things that the rest of us wouldn't have the courage to do. But it's how he approaches playing a drunk that blew my mind.

First of all, he doesn't drink. At all.

Second, his feeling is that when people are really drunk, they're not stumbling all over the place and crashing into walls. They're trying their best to hold it together. So the more Lahey keeps it barely together, the funnier it is when he finally does fall down a staircase. It's so effective.

Pat Roach was an executive at a bottled-water company when *Trailer Park Boys* started. During the first couple of seasons, he just cashed in vacation days to shoot his Randy scenes. Finally, as the third season was about to start, his boss at the water company gave him an ultimatum.

"Pat, I don't think you can be an executive here and the guy on TV with no shirt on. You're going to have to choose."

Fortunately for Canadian television history, he chose the show. Here's the best part. A year later, his boss came to him and asked if he would help train the new executives—*as Randy*!

Pat loses weight every winter and has to go into cheeseburger training in the spring. For optimal bulbousness, he'll eat two or three double cheeseburgers a day for several weeks leading up to taping. The best part about his stomach is that you can't even tell he has it if you're standing behind him. He's a slender-hipped anomaly.

John and Pat's relationship on the road is adorable. Pat books the flights, John drives the rental car. Pat arranges meals, John deals with venues. They even call each other Randy and Lahey. Their real-life banter is as endearing as their characters.

Lake or Fake?

Canada has so many crazy names for lakes, many of them sound like a joke. Grab yer two-piece and yer two-four and guess if these guys are lakes or fakes.

1. Molson Lake
2. Lake Chachi
3. Cabonga Reservoir
4. Shart Lake
5. Peter Pond Lake
6. Lac Googlie
7. Gary Lake
8. Lake Darrell
9. Lac Swassis/Saucisse
10. Lake Winnipegosis
11. Peckerwood Lake
12. Pickle Lake
13. God's Lake
14. Lake Phaneuf
15. Lake Pekwachna-maykoskwask-waypinwanik
16. Lake Titicaca

Numbers 2, 4, 6, 8, 9 and 14 are FAKE. Numbers 1, 10, 13 and 15 are lakes in Manitoba; number 3 is in Quebec; number 5 is in Saskatchewan; number 7 is in Nunavut; number 11 is in Arkansas; number 12 is in Ontario; and number 16 is in the Andes, between Bolivia and Peru.

Camp or Crap?

A variation on Lake or Fake is Camp or Crap. Camps are supposed to have weird names, but are some of these too ridiculous to be real? Get your happy campers to take a stab at these:

1. **Camp Coodaloogoo (Skiff Lake, New Brunswick)**
2. **Camp Watchalista Counselah (Winkler, Manitoba)**
3. **Camp Itchialeggey (Falcon Lake, Manitoba)**
4. **Camp Trustafunda (Chestermere, Alberta)**
5. **Camp Crotchadoo (Stormer Lake, Ontario)**
6. **Camp Leavem Malone (Duncan, British Columbia)**
7. **Camp Touch This (Michipicoten Provincial Park, Ontario)**
8. **Camp Getchi Clothesoff (Mahone Bay, Nova Scotia)**
9. **Camp Ing (Carpenter Lake, British Columbia)**
10. **Camp Catcha Virus (Sars Lake)**

Trick question. They're all fake.

A rare piece of *Trailer Park* trivia for you while we're on the subject. Philadelphia Collins, aka the Mustard Tiger, was played with vigour by an actor named Richard Collins, who sadly isn't with us anymore.

Phil's burps were legendary in volume and scope. I'm semi-proud to say they were actually mine. Clattenburg and the sound department would roll tape and wait while I chugged a can of Diet Coke and hopped up and down for a moment or two to get things going.

The Movie Trick and Manitoba Memories

Taggart

When you're a musician on the road, life slows down a bit during the twenty-two-hour stretches in between the ninety minutes you spend onstage. You sleep as long as you can, see the sights (even that gets old if you're in a new city every day for two years straight) and watch movies—shitloads of movies. I remember being in Winnipeg with OLP when *Pulp Fiction* came out. It was playing at the theatre in the Polo Park mall. This was a great way to kill a night off, and we were pretty burnt out from a long run of touring.

We got to the mall and saw a lineup all the way out the door and down the escalators. Apparently, half of Winnipeg wanted to see this Quentin Tarantino joint as much as we did. His first feature-length film, *Reservoir Dogs*, had been a cult classic that paved the way for a perfect buildup of hype to entice this ram-jammed crowd in Polo Park. All hope for an enjoyable night out at the movies seemed to be lost. Except that I remembered my dad had told me about a classic trick to get into films for free.

He used to use it on busy nights in the Bronx in the '50s. He would go with fellas in his boyhood gang, the Junior Bacooches, wait until the early movie let out, and then slowly walk backwards through the middle of the crowd coming out. Not all at once— that would look too obvious. Just one at a time, three steps back, one step forward. People don't notice it because they're in a rush to leave. So you kind of wedge your way, at a reasonable backwards pace, into the lobby, and then through the ticket gate, which is always unmanned. A key point: you have to make sure you're in the centre of the crowd and not on the fringes.

I went first to prove that the gambit worked, and when the others noticed that I hadn't come back out, they followed suit. It worked like a charm! The key is that it has to be a busy night. You can't do it otherwise—you'll never make it without the crowd.

Anyway, we got in and had plenty of time to buy snacks and drinks—hell, we even had president's choice of seats! The kids cleaning up from the last showing just saw us as eager ticket-holders, awaiting the start of the film.

What a great movie it was, too! We had a fantastic night. I went a couple more times to see it—paying in full, because it was worth every dollar. But I'll tell you, every time I see a clip from *Pulp Fiction*, I think of that great move that Ronnie bequeathed upon me. Thanks, Dad!

When Jono and I played Winnipeg, we were lucky enough to stop at Stella's, a fantastic breakfast spot. It was a great move, we had a super-cool waitress who cracked us up and the food was fresh and tasty. I even picked up a jar of their famous jam to send to Jay Onrait as a fun gift of Canadianity, but when I was flying home from Saskatoon, they wouldn't let me take it on the plane! They said it was going to the food bank, so at least it wasn't getting tossed out. Sorry, Jay!

Played a festival in 1994 in Gimli, Manitoba, called Sunfest. I remember the Odds being incredibly tight live. They did a classic version of "So What'cha Want" by the Beastie Boys. Seeing Stompin' Tom Connors crushing a dart by himself was pretty classic—just taking in another day at the rodeo. He smoked like a hitcher. *Rolling Stone* style. Just a legend on a dart break.

That whole day felt pretty Canadian. The Watchmen played, as well as 54-40, and the MC was Father Guido Sarducci. I've played a lot of festivals, but that was the first time playing with a bunch of big Canadian bands. I'm pretty sure that was the last time I saw Father Guido (played by Don Novello) do anything.

Burton for Certain

In honour of Burtonius Maximus—the great Burton Cummings— we played a game where we read quotes to each other and had to guess whether it was "Burton for Certain." See how you do:

1. "Winnipeg. Man, what a place to grow up. Just hangin' around, mostly listening to rock and roll on the radio. The radio was fabulous, man. Every night it was rock and roll, rock and roll. The best of all of it: Elvis, Buddy Holly, Chuck Berry, Fats Domino, Little Richard. It was rock and roll, man!"

2. "The songs. It's the songs, I mean, it sounds like they tell me what to do. I write the song, but, uh, it was better the first time we talked about it."

3. "I'm delighted to hear somebody reads those. I've been involved in putting some out and some of them—callous publishers—believe that coffee-table books are really furniture, that nobody actually reads them at all, but you do. At least you look at the pictures."

4. "I'm very pleased with the production. The band had a good night and I thought my night was pretty good too. The sound was good and it looks pretty good too."

5. "I've done all that, you know. I'm not really into that whole 'running with the pack' scene. I mean, I go to my lawyer's office, I bump into Gregory Peck, Warren Beatty, Steve McQueen and (Mick) Jagger and guys like that and they're just like anybody else, you know?"

6. "The music and lyrics are often written at the same time. Sometimes the chords themselves will beget certain words."

7. "Within the next few years, from what I hear in the wind, they're going to be able to bypass tape. They're now storing mixes digitally into a computer brain and having a readout. So the tape will be eliminated, and you're actually eliminating the middleman so that every record will be sort of like a direct-to-disc pressing. It's a phenomenal step ahead, as far as the recording industry goes."

8. "My wife pounded on my studio door, like a lunatic, and I was afraid that someone was breaking into my house. And she grabs me and takes me upstairs and Manny is singing on *Jimmy Kimmel*."

9. "I think one of the problems with historians in Canada is there's no tradition of popular history. Nobody's telling you what it was really like, they're telling you what the great currents in history were. They don't tell you what the smell of things were like, what people wore or how they looked or how they felt. I don't want to sound egotistical here; I don't want to blow my own horn but I've done the kind of a job that should have been done years ago in this country about this extremely important war."

1, 5, 7: Burton for Certain; 2: Neil Young; 4: Gino Vannelli; 6: Alanis Morissette; 8: Dan Hill; 3, 9: Trick answer: Pierre Berton

Taggart's Top Five "Cleaning Up the Cottage" Jams

Many jams make light work. Fire these on while you're chasing dust bunnies around your place at Lake Winnipegosis on May 2-4.

5. "Ready to Start" • Arcade Fire
4. "No Sugar Tonight" • The Guess Who
3. "The Lion Sleeps Tonight" • The Tokens
2. "Seasons in the Sun" • Terry Jacks
1. "Four Strong Winds" • Neil Young

Manitoba Gotta Do's

DESTROY perogies at the Forks.

CRUSH your weight in meat in a relaxed dining atmosphere from a bygone time at Rae & Jerry's Steak House.

PEEL up to North Knife Lake Lodge. If you're a fishermafk, this place is a must. Charters start in Thompson for an expedition that can land you a fish the size of your own leg. Plus, the Hip have a song called "Thomson Girl," so that's a Canadianity double double.

OGLE animals at Assiniboine Park Zoo. Great family spot.

Hay, Saskatchewan! Wheat's Up?

Bahd Bands

The Waltons

The Northern Pikes

The Sheepdogs

The Age of Electric

The Deep Dark Woods

Five Notable Bahds

Graham DeLaet. A bearded bahd outta Weyburn. Burning up the PGA.

Leslie Nielsen. Growing up in the harsh prairie winters must've contributed to Leslie's dry sense of humour. From *Airplane!* to the *Naked Gun* trilogy, he's consistently one of the funniest actors Canada has ever produced. Even funnier: his brother Erik was the deputy prime minister of Canada!

Steve Nash. A generation of Canadian kids took to the game of Nash-ketball because Steve paved the way by charging the lane against the biggest names in the game. But remember, it's our game. (Shout-out to James Naismith and Heritage Minutes.)

Ryan Getzlaf. NHLer, another sizable feller. A huge part of any

Canadian team on the world stage in the past decade or so. Brother Chris Getzlaf is a CFLer feller.

Tommy Douglas. Thanks for the free health care, bahd! Kiefer Sutherland sure won the grandfather sweepstakes with TD.

The Birthplace of Bahddism May Be Saskatchewan

Taggart

As you head west and spend some time in Saskatchewan, you'll find so many warm-hearted people.

I've played Regina and Saskatoon many times. I'll always remember going to the bathroom after a show at Channel One in Regina, and there was a true bahd standing in the urinal beside me. He said nice things about the show and chatted about the night. I enjoyed the conversation, but I was amazed by the way he had his arms folded above his barrel the whole time. That's the first time I saw that special move. I was impressed.

This was back in the day of band houses. You would stay at a house that the club rented instead of at a hotel. Some places were too greasy to stay in, like the one that Crocks N Rolls in Thunder Bay had. I slept in the van instead. The Channel One house wasn't bad, though—it was more rustic and had more vibe than filth.

I enjoyed the flat landscape and dry weather. It was also the first time that I required lip balm twenty-four hours a day. I had lips like Steve McQueen in *Papillon* as soon as I got out of Winnipeg.

Truck stops can sometimes be pretty greasy, anywhere in Canada. I love reading the bathroom walls as you travel the country. Sometimes you find awful limericks or jokes; sometimes cowardly lines that scream out the insecurities of the person who penned them. I'll never forget one that I saw on a bathroom door at a Saskatchewan Husky: "Steak knife, Steve Kotchey is a Chief!" I don't know what the hell it means, or whether it's a rhyme or a statement, but it has somehow locked itself into my brain, never to be forgotten. The poetry of the road dumpers.

Jono and I found the great Saskatchewan to be the ground zero of Canadianity, I think mostly because they are truly happy with what they have: the 'Riders and potash. Everyone's a bahd, no matter where you go. The support they show for the CFL is blinding bahddism. NFL? What NFL?

Driving through the Prairies is a trip. So wide and open. There are no secrets on the landscape, nowhere to hide, nowhere to run. If it's windy, though, it's pretty scary. When Jono and I were going from Winnipeg to Regina on our live *TnT* tour, it was really windy. The gusts felt like we were gonna get burled right off the road. A couple of days later we heard about a band getting blown off the road in their van and trailer on that same stretch. Luckily, they weren't hurt, the poor bahds. I don't envy bahds who need to drive back and forth along that highway. Burl safe!

Prairie Companions

Torrens

Not unlike in Manitoba, hustlers in Saskatchewan represent. Case in point: fans of the Saskatchewan Roughriders buy more merchandise than fans of all the other teams combined.

When Jeremy and I arrived at Amigos Cantina in

Saskatoon for the last stop on the western swing of our tour, we couldn't believe how many bahds were there—350, according to some. That's a lot when you consider *TnT* is really just a phone conversation that people eavesdrop on.

Remember the scene in *Fargo* where Steve Buscemi and that blond guy were driving down to the city, and Buscemi's character couldn't understand how the other guy could stay so quiet? That was Taggart and me on our Comedy & Canadianity tour through Saskatchewan. It didn't help that we'd been doing a string of late nights, with lots of talking and the time change. So I was actually losing my voice.

It was also the geography that left me speechless, though. You hear so much about how flat it is and how far you can see, but until you've driven it, it's hard to comprehend.

We were there at the time of year when hoarfrost covers the trees in an ominous white shellac, as though the scenery has literally been frozen in time. It's hauntingly beautiful.

Very few musicians I've heard capture the spirit of Saskatchewan the way Jason Plumb does. His band, the Waltons, was wicked live. I've always seen him as equal parts stellar songwriter and earworm farmer. His voice isn't fancy, but it's—to steal from one of his song titles—steeped in "Truth and Beauty." Same with my bahd Connie Kaldor, a folksinger originally from Saskatchewan who can suck the tears out of your head with one heartfelt opening note. There also isn't a better "vamper" on the planet Earth. She can riff for two hundred bars at the start of a song and not only accompany herself on the piano but deliver joke after joke at the same time. That's a skill in itself.

The best jokes often come when you're not expecting them. A few years ago, I was in the airport in Saskatoon buying a pack of gum and the woman working behind the counter started to practically hyperventilate upon seeing me. I tried to play it cool and give off the "just a regular guy buying gum" vibe—the one that requires no effort because that's exactly what I am.

"I can't believe it's you," she said.

"Well, it is." Trying to play it cool.

"My friends won't believe me when I tell them I met you. Can I ask you a question?"

"Sure," I said. "Anything at all!" Trying to sound super-open and approachable (because I actually am).

"What's it like being on *Coronation Street*?"

I smiled weakly. "Fun."

The fact that I didn't have a British accent didn't seem to throw her off the scent.

Pretty easy to stay grounded when you work in Canadian showbiz.

When my daughter was almost three, she was in the living room, where the TV was on. I was in the kitchen doing dishes. She was suddenly very excited. "Daddy! Daddy's on TV! *Daddy's on TV!*" I ran into the room, beaming with pride.

She was watching *Ellen*.

Now that she's five, she's catching on to what I do for a living. We were in Sobeys recently, and a man recognized me from *Trailer Park Boys*. We chatted for a few minutes, and when he walked away, she looked at me sideways.

"Why did that man call you 'J-Ruff'?" Cute. It's a weird moment in a man's life when your kid calls you by the name of a fake rapper from a TV show.

Word is slowly getting out at school that Sugar-Daisy's daddy was on *Wipeout Canada*. Or Indigo's ol' man hosts *Game On* on YTV.

But to them, I'm just Daddy. Well, the Great Dadoo. That's the name I've given myself. It's better than the Town Crier.

Everywhere we go, I ask them if they heard people chanting, "Great Dadoo! Great Dadoo!" behind our backs. They never can.

Once, on the sly, I asked the dude working at Dairy Queen to walk by our table, stop, point and say, "Hey, aren't you the Great Dadoo?" He did it and it worked perfectly. Their minds were blown.

Until they saw me slip him a twenty.

Bahd Ambassador
Andrea Dion

Andrea, a news anchor at Global, spent some time working in Regina and offered these solid tips for the town that rhymes with fun.

- **La Bodega.** Always has half-priced wine, and has a veranda patio and rooftop patio.
- **Leopold's Tavern.** Kind of a grungy vibe. Small setting, but always packed. Good music, craft beer and awesome pub food.
- **Victoria's Tavern.** Where everyone goes to drink. Good bar staff, small space too. They also have a good outdoor patio, which they keep heated until the snow flies. You'll see all ages there and constant turnover all night. Good beer selection.
- **Fat Badger.** Best place for people who want to dance.
- **Crave.** A wine bar on the pricier side, but worth it. They have chefs there that have won those gold-medal plate comps. And an excellent wine and cocktail list.
- **Flip Eatery.** Good cocktails. Kind of has a cafeteria setup for seating.

- **Willow on Wascana.** More expensive also, but lots of fresh product and seafood. Overlooks Wascana Lake and is on top of the boathouse.
- **Sprout** and **Fresh & Sweet.** The best breakfasts (the latter serves homemade white-chocolate-chip banana bread French toast).

Canadianity

Taggart

What do I think Canadianity is? Put it this way. It's a hell of a lot easier to be nice than to be a cock to everyone. Being friendly to new people you meet requires easy lifting. People from Saskatchewan get it. "How's she goin'?" or "Have a good one" are great examples of Canadian greetings that make you feel accepted and cared about when you hear them, definitely not coldness or arrogance, but they are just simple sentences that ward off consequence. They keep it quick and clean, easily getting the ball of conversation over to your side of the net. In reality, there's actually a veiled strength there. Though we appear respectful, we're actually quite guarded with our personal space and would rather take in your information and hold back our own until we know who we're talking to.

That's Canadianity.

The most Canadian I've ever felt has to be turning over the car engine in freezing February. Sitting, slowly feeling tortured by the creeping cold. When you're a kid, it's getting on an early bus for school, second or third on the route, the bus just burlin' like a frozen skeleton, waiting to heat up. That's one of my most prominent memories since I was born. Being cold, en route somewhere. Dealing with it, even the blessed feeling of getting over it and actually enjoying myself in the cold. I never played league hockey, but I always had a blast messing around on a backyard or public rink, almost enjoying the cold. Not anymore. I'm like a chihuahua.

I spent a lot of winters touring or recording away in warmer climates, even when I spent a few winters in Hawaii and LA and a rainy one in Vancouver, which is gloomy and shitty for months straight, and on the day you're thinking about packing bags to leave, it's sunny and you forget how shitty it was. Through all that, the avoidance of a cold, snowy winter turned off my inner furnace that I'd been equipped with at birth. I need to go full-on Farley Mowat and get it back.

I also feel pretty Canadian when I'm not in Canada, like at the Salt Lake 2002 Olympic gold-medal hockey game. I was lucky enough to get a ticket for the game and had a few days off while recording the *Gravity* album in Vancouver. I hopped on a flight and got settled in Salt Lake City. Seeing a large group of bahds in line to get into the arena, including the legendary Walter Gretzky, who was right with me in line, I was with my great friend John Kawaja (he got me the ticket) and his wife, Laura, and a couple thousand other Canadians who were right fired up for the game. We had corner seats right at ice level. The way Canada played was so entertaining, never letting up on the US and winning easily. It felt pretty awesome beating them at home. We went over to the after-party to try to find a way in. I saw Cujo—goalie Curtis Joseph—whom I'd met a few times and can confirm that he's a bahd. He got us into the party and it was spectacular! The whole team and coaching staff just getting right into things. Everyone, from Steve Yzerman to Wayne Gretzky, just giddy as school kids. Even Steve Nash, who was playing for the NBA's

Phoenix Suns at the time, had to be there to experience the joy. It was quite a time.

I gotta say, skating in a classic barn feels pretty Canadian. The drafty cold ones with the old trophies and alumni pics in the lobby. Maybe you'll get lucky and they'll have one of the classic hot chocolate/chicken soup machines. Remember those? Greasy yellow water with green flecks that are somehow supposed to make the drink resemble a nice, hearty chicken soup . . . that has overtones of hot chocolate. Not quite as bad as the hot chocolate that had undertones of chicken broth and green flecks. The ice is always perfect in these rinks, though. Old-school masters on the Zamboni. The formula for mint ice on lock. Heavy Canadianity.

Watching *The Hilarious House of Frightenstein* on a Saturday morning felt like a pretty hard Canadianity move. That show was absolutely classic. Billy Van was one of the greats. His talent and ability was second to none. Van portrayed almost every character in the show, probably to save money, since the show had to have a tiny budget. My favourite character was the Wolfman, the DJ who threw on classic jams and then danced as a silhouette on a psychedelic screen of video feedback. Jams like "Born to Be Wild," or "I Want to Take You Higher" by Sly and the Family Stone. He'd hold a guitar that was literally an axe and bring out the other *Frightenstein* bahds to dance with him throughout the entire song. So classic.

That show was made for CHCH in Hamilton (home also to the Ed Allen exercise show), all 130 episodes of it. Apparently they only had Vincent Price for four days, during which they taped about fourteen segments at a cost of thirteen grand. Price said he liked the project because it was for kids. I gotta say, his presence in the House really tied the whole show together.

It bums me out that Billy Van hasn't been more celebrated. People need to know how great he was. At least put the show out again with the full Wolfman jams.

I love Canada during fall. I was a massive fan of Halloween—it relieved the uneasiness of a new school year. Seeing all the decorations and community spirit always got me going. Growing up in southern Ontario has its benefits. The colour of the trees in September and October is one of the best reasons to live here.

My favourite area in fall has to be the Headwaters area, just north of Toronto. All those beautiful rivers like the Nottawasaga, the Boyne, the Rouge and the Mad, all meeting up in the glorious watershed of the headwaters. The abundance of fresh water created this beautiful landscape and incredible soil. If you get a chance, go for a walk in Horning's Mills, Honeywood or my old stomping grounds, Mansfield, and you'll be blown away by the beauty of this treasured space. I got real lucky growing up in that area. It's so fresh and awake there in the fall, you can almost hear all the natural preparation for winter. Canadianity at its best!

Bahd Ambassadors

Maple Syrup Shots

Neil and Dave from the podcast *Maple Syrup Shots* (named after our *TnT* game!) have these solid tips for Saskatoon.

- **Winston's English Pub.** Best beer selection in Saskatoon (seventy-two taps!)
- **Meewasin Valley.** Great area to walk and take in Saskatoon's beauty.
- **Mardi Gras Grill.** Louisiana-style cuisine in the heart of the Prairies!

- **Wanuskewin Heritage Park.** A great place to take in nature and learn some of the history of Canada's indigenous peoples.

Bahd Ambassador
Jay Onrait

Anchor and bestselling author Jay Onrait got his start pounding smaller broadcast markets in the Prairies before landing at TSN in Toronto. One half of Jay & Dan (he plays the challenging role of "Jay"), the super-popular TSN bahd-casters, Jay was kind enough to take some time out from husbandhood, dadhood and listening to obscure bands to offer these suggestions for where to eat and drink in Saskatoon.

When I was living in Toronto, one of the things that used to make me truly upset was when a friend or colleague would travel to a city in the Prairies for work, and then come back saying something like "I couldn't find *anywhere* to eat but bad chain restaurants. I am *not* a fan of that town!"

Could there be a lazier statement? If Canadian bahd John Catucci has taught us anything on his hit Food Network show *You Gotta Eat Here*, it's that this country is absolutely filled with amazing places to eat, drink and party in whatever city or town you find yourself in. All you have to do is ask a bahd who lives there.

So if someone asks me where to have a drink or a bite in Saskatoon, where I lived in the late '90s and love to visit to this day, I usually say the **Yard & Flagon** or the **Crazy Cactus** for drinks, and either of *Top Chef Canada* winner Dale MacKay's two amazing restaurants, **Ayden Kitchen & Bar** or **Little Grouse on the Prairie**.

Games Little People Play

We were talking on a poddy about the ridiculous games we used to play as kids. It worries me that, nowadays, kids don't have to use their imaginations to invent games the way we did. Games like Chuck the Boot, which Taggart used to play with his brother Jet. You'd sit on opposite beds with your legs wide open and take turns chucking a boot at each other's midsection. Only rule was you couldn't move if it was coming right for your . . . area.

We love it when people are inspired to write in and share their own bits of Canadianity with us. For some reason, dumb kids games really struck a chord. Here are just a few of the submissions we got. Not surprisingly, some of the best ones come from the Prairies, where there's nothing but space and time to fill.

In Indian Head, Saskatchewan, we used to play a game on my buddy's farm where we stacked up old tires on the end of an old rusty auger. Then we would climb up to the top of the auger to bring it down. As a few of us held the auger down, one person would let go, shooting the others up. One time we thought it would be funny to all let go and send our skinniest friend to the top. He couldn't hang on when it banged to a stop at the top. He fell pretty hard. There wasn't a very good grip, because it's just round—hahaha. Most fun we ever had growing up. "Wanna go play on the auger?"

Kevin

We weren't kids per se when we played this game, but I think it's still worth sharing. My bahds Nick and Jon and I were hanging out one day with nothing do when we were eighteen or nineteen.

We found an old Snapple bottle and a long piece of speaker wire at the side of a road, so Jon tied the wire around the neck of the bottle and began dragging it behind him and pretended the bottle was his pet dog. It was funny at first, but the joke went on for hours as we walked around our neighbourhood. Finally, the bottle hit a curb a little hard and it smashed, and Jon cradled the broken bits in his hands and feigned sobbing while people walked by, aghast. Once he stopped sobbing, I'm pretty sure we went to Jon's parents' place and got banged up at three in the afternoon.

A few days later, Jon showed up at my door with a new bottle and the same speaker wire "leash," but he managed not to smash his new pet while we walked around that day.

Warren

When I was around ten, a buddy and I used to play a game where we would take turns throwing rocks at each other while the other person shielded himself with a trash can lid. We would go into the gravel alley behind his house and stand about ten yards away from each other. One person would yell out the type of gun (rifle, machine gun, spread, etc.), and the other person would have to shield himself from the oncoming rock(s). A rifle meant you threw one rock, a machine gun was several rocks one at a time, and the spread gun was a handful of rocks thrown all at once. It was a blast, we were dumb, and it's a miracle we still have two functioning eyes.

Philip

When I was younger, me and a group of bahds used to play a game we called "price check." Basically, we'd set up a pop can about ten to fifteen metres away and throw rocks at it. The goal was to knock the can over, but your "award" for hitting the can was getting to run over and set the can back up, while the rest of the group ripped rocks at you and chanted "Make that fucker pay the price." Hence the name "price check." Oh, and a rule was you couldn't wear a shirt. We played this game right into young adulthood and sometimes had fifteen to twenty people playing at a time. Great times.

Graham

I have got a couple of doozies for ya! The arrow game you guys talked about—shooting an arrow straight up into the air—me and my cousin did that. But we got slightly banged up and would play in the dark, losing sight of the arrow. We'd take off in one direction, hoping it would be away from where the arrow would strike the ground. More than once we would stop and the arrow would land terrifyingly close. Good times. The other one we played was with the old sharp-tipped lawn darts. We'd stand like twenty metres [apart] (gotta keep the Canadianity strong) and throw the darts, with the goal being to either make the other person move or have it land between their legs. Had a couple close calls on that one!

Deaner

Saskatchewan Gotta Do's

CRUSH some drinks and get nuts at the Crazy Cactus in Saskatoon. Tell them Jay and Dan sent ya!

RIP the family around the Wascana Centre park in Regina for a beauty of a walk.

WHISTLE back in time and say hi to Scotty the *T. rex*, the 65-million-year-old dinobahd in Eastend.

Alberta: Choice Cuts and Truck Nuts

Bahd Bands

Ian Tyson

Jann Arden

Emerson Drive

The Stampeders

Stereos

Corb Lund

Paul Brandt

Five Notable Bahds

Bret "The Hitman" Hart. Wrestling legend from a wrestling dynasty. *Jonovision* guest. Perfect gentleman.

W.O. Mitchell. One of our most beloved authors. Posed the question plaguing Canadians for generations: *Who Has Seen the Wind?*

Kurt Browning. Four-time world champion figure skater.

Michael J. Fox. The actor of our generation. *Family Ties* and *Back to the Future*. Made skateboarding, guitar playing and—somehow—even being a Republican cool.

Nellie McClung. Women's rights activist known for using her great sense of humour in arguments. Smart and funny. Solid Canadian combo.

Bonus Bahd

Conrad Bain. The dad from *Diff'rent Strokes* was born in Alberta!

The Game of Our Lives

Torrens

People are always curious as to how I became an Edmonton Oilers fan. When I was a kid, fabled CBC broadcaster Peter Gzowski spent a year with the Oilers, when they were new to the NHL and Wayne Gretzky, Paul Coffey, Mark Messier, Kevin Lowe and company were all kids. Like, eighteen-year-old kids.

Gzowski's book was called *The Game of Our Lives*, and it became my bible. It combined my obsession over the game with my curiosity/nosiness. The behind-the-scenes aspect was intoxicating to me, and I devoured every anecdote, from on-ice drills to pranks played on the plane.

It's interesting to reread the book now, knowing what they went on to accomplish as individuals and as a team. But that's how my lifelong Oilers fandom was cemented.

I got to meet Peter a few times over the years, and I'm pretty sure I told him every single time just how much I loved the book. If you knew him at all, you can imagine how uncomfortable that made him.

Last year, I went to a game at Rexall Place. My first one ever. (In the days when it was Northlands Coliseum, I didn't have the kind of bank to make the trip from PEI.) Tom Gazzola, the Oilers' video host, heard I was coming and asked who my favourite player was. I thought about it for a minute. When I was a kid, it was Andy Moog, because we were both portly goalies. These days, it was Dave Semenko, I told him. Because we're both used to playing supporting roles.

When I arrived, the team presented me with an official Oilers jersey emblazoned with "27" (Semenko's number) and "TORRENS" on the back. I had to really concentrate not to cry. Pal-berta's full of bahds.

Tom Gazzola, Chris Wescott and Ryan Frankson

As the video crew for the Edmonton Oilers, Tom Gazzola, Chris Westcott and Ryan Frankson have their fingers on the pulse of what's crackin' in E-town. Here are a couple of their favourite hotspots.

- **Tres Carnales Taquería.** Solid Mexican.
- **Pizzeria Rosso.** Food and drinks.
- **Woodwork Downtown.** Food and cocktails.
- **Meat (off Whyte Avenue).** Meat.

Banff Bahd

Taggart

I've had some great times in the Alberta mountains. Back in the mid-'90s, OLP was sidelined for a week (Maida threw out his back and couldn't move), so I went skiing at Sunshine Village in Banff for a bit— ripping up some slopes and falling on my ass continually while trying to snowboard. I was never meant for that means of transportation. High risk of wrist and ass-bone injuries. No thanks.

I went to the best stag ever in Jasper Park Lodge. My bahd Tim Palmer was getting married, and his brother, Al—also a good bahd—was the golf pro at JPL, so he dialled us into a beautiful lodge, where we had such a great time golfing and walking around, enjoying the multiple mountain vistas. That place is the ultimate relaxation spot. Every inch of it is gorgeous.

Bahd Ambassadors
Jay Onrait and Reid Wilkins

TSN anchor Jay Onrait is a native of Athabasca, Alberta, so he finds plenty of comfort food in his home province. So does his good friend Reid Wilkins, host of *Inside Sports* and the Oilers hockey show on 630 CHED radio. Thanks to Reid for sharing his recommendations for where to eat and drink in Edmonton.

- **Black Dog Freehouse.** Great "dive bar" on Whyte Avenue. Good spot to listen to live music and meet folks of all ages and lifestyles. Stickiest countertops in the west!
- **Cook County Saloon.** Underage two-steppers abound.
- **Corso#32/Bar Bricco/Uccellino.** Three Italian restaurants side by side on Jasper Avenue offering a variety of dishes. Get a hearty plate of homemade pasta at Corso#32, or head to Uccellino for some tapas. When Corso#32 opened, you'd have to wait months to get a reservation.
- **Northern Chicken.** New addition to the Edmonton food scene. Co-owner Matt Phillips grew up loving fried chicken. Now he's

perfected the recipe and serves it. The Doritos mac 'n' cheese is a must-have side dish.

- **Rostizado.** Same gentlemen who own Tres Carnales. This is their option for more formal Modern Mexican cuisine. The chicken, beef and pork platters are all delicious. The roasted cauliflower and sweet onions are perfect sides. Located across from Rogers Place.

- **The Lingnan/Chicken for Lunch.** Owned by the Quon family, these Edmonton institutions earned national attention when featured on a TV series called *The Family Restaurant*. The Lingnan offers Chinese dishes for all tastes, while Chicken for Lunch is one of the city's busiest lunch spots. Order quick or risk losing your spot in line!

- **Underground Tap & Grill.** Best beer list in the city, with seventy-two rotating taps featuring craft brews from around Alberta and the world. Excellent food menu too. I recommend the bacon/avocado grilled cheese sandwich.

- **Highlevel Diner.** Historic spot near the University of Alberta at the south end of the landmark High Level Bridge. Six cinnamon buns to go? Yes, please!

- **Costco.** $1.50 hot dogs.

#GetMeBackFromFortMac

Torrens

In the spring of 2016, a wildfire unlike any I'd ever seen ravaged Alberta. It was out of control for several weeks, and though most of it raged in relatively uninhabited parts of the province, Canadians held their breath as it danced around Fort McMurray a couple of times but retreated.

Then it didn't. Winds changed and so did the intensity of the fire. Within hours, the fire engulfed the town and panic-stricken residents grabbed what they could and did what they had to in order to get out of there.

Of course, in this day and age, most of the people fleeing were able to capture video of their harrowing escapes. The images were terrifying. Flames licking the sides of their vehicle as they inched their way out of the danger zone, like a morbid parade, praying they didn't run out of gas. Almost in the same way that your brain couldn't process planes flying into buildings on 9/11, images of cars driving through walls of flame were inconceivable.

There was one video in particular of a mom driving through a tunnel of fire with sparks landing on her windshield. You could hear her kids in the back asking hopeful questions, wanting reassurance, and the tension in her voice as she tried to calmly respond.

It really rattled me. Thinking about having to flee the place we love with the people we love through atrocious circumstances was inconceivable. It was like a Hollywood blockbuster, but real.

I knew I wanted to do something. But what could I really do so many miles away?

Being a father has made me two things: wimpier and braver. I'm wimpier because I don't want anything to happen to me that will leave the girls without a father, but braver in that I'll do anything to protect them.

Fort McMurray is home away from home to so many East Coast sons and daughters, fathers and mothers who sacrificed a lot to provide for their families. They went where the work was and left families behind so that they could give them a better life.

I can relate to that.

They're also people with a good work ethic, who don't want handouts and are happy to put in the time to make a wage to put food on their table back home. It's very admirable, really.

Soon the stories started to emerge. A family that had lost everything had no place to stay. A couple and their dogs were stranded at the airport. A grandmother who'd been helping her daughter had to flee and had lost contact with her.

Home.

These people had lost their home.

Home.

People rallied immediately in typical Canadian fashion. Every story of hurt was countered by a story of hope. It was heartbreaking and heartwarming at the same time.

But I just kept thinking about home. What it means to me and what losing it would feel like. So I put out a tweet saying that if anyone from the East Coast was affected by the fire and wanted to come home but didn't have the means, I'd help arrange their travel.

That was it. With no real plan other than my sincere offer, I decided that it didn't matter if I didn't know anyone in Fort McMurray or have any family there. What mattered was that people were in need and I wanted to help in my own small way.

Boy, did I underestimate the response.

I wrestle with using social media as a place to do community work. It's obviously a great way to reach a great number of people, but the notion that what I was doing could somehow be perceived as being for personal gain grossed me out.

Ultimately, though, I just decided that I knew the reason I was making the offer. And I didn't have anything to promote or gain from the exposure.

The initiative took off like a rocket. I started getting messages right away. "Can you help me?" "Can you help my parents?" "Can I put you in touch with a shelter that has lots of people who need to get somewhere?"

Yes, sure, I said. I just kept saying yes, secretly not really knowing how I could manage to help more than a few.

I used my own personal points to book three or four tickets home. Then I used cash to buy a couple more.

But the demand kept coming. Almost every single person who got in touch with me started by saying, "You have to know if I had any other option, I wouldn't be contacting you." It broke my heart.

So I put the ask out: Who had Aeroplan miles they could part with? Out of nowhere, people were sending messages saying, "I have two thousand—they're yours if you can use them!"

Soon people were offering drives, couches and gas to those who were driving home. We helped get a couple of Via Rail tickets for people who couldn't fly. I was pairing this person who needed a lift with that person who needed gas money.

Comedian Ron James asked what he could do. So did Gerry Dee. I paired them each directly with families that needed some help. Ron got the tickets booked and the evacuees on their way. Gerry even booked a mother and son a room at Pearson airport so they had somewhere to go during their five-hour layover.

Hockey legend Hayley Wickenheiser and I connected on Twitter and she said the Calgary contingent could mobilize quickly—they had things figured out after the devastating Alberta flood of 2013. As if I didn't already think she was the very definition of Canadianity. I love her.

Slowly things were coming together. I set up a charitable pool at Aeroplan called #GetMeBackFromFortMac where folks could donate their miles.

We were managing. Booking and buying tickets for those in need. But they just kept coming. "It's me, my two daughters, my best friend and her son." Story after story. All legit, all worthy, all complicated.

It was also becoming clear in the days that followed just what a big undertaking it was going to be to get Fort Mac back on its feet again. There was major widespread damage. Even the optimists were starting to realize they wouldn't be back to work for quite some time. So they emerged from shelters and friends' houses, wondering about the possibility of getting help with tickets home.

By this time, most of the flights out were overbooked and our miles stash was dwindling.

Then rocker Joel Plaskett donated 200,000 of them.

Gat dang, I love this country. There were concerts and bake sales and offers of cottages. Even the politicians seemed to be getting along. It's the oldest clich-eh that tough times bring people together, but boy, it's true.

In the end, we booked more than fifty flights back to the East Coast for stranded Fort Mac fire victims. I was really proud, mostly of this great country and how we can come together in times of need.

Two weeks after we booked the last ticket, I got an email from one of the people I'd booked a flight for early on. He needed to get back out to Fort Mac. Work had called him to come clean up, but he didn't have the means. I used the last of the points to score him and another guy tickets back out there.

Months later, I bumped into Rick Mercer at a CBC fall launch function. He told me his mother had asked him if he planned to donate miles to help people get home from Fort Mac. In typical saucy fashion, he explained to her that if he donated his miles, she'd never get to go anywhere.

Man, he's funny.

Microphonies

A game we called Microphonies asks the question, Which of the following is a real cover band? Let's start with good Alberta boys Nickelback.

1. **Poor Man Stealin' (Nickelback)**

2. **Are We Them (R.E.M.)**

3. **Runs in Your Hoses (Guns N' Roses)**

4. **Björn Again (ABBA)**

5. **AC/DShe (all-female AC/DC)**

6. **Counting Cornrows (Counting Crows)**

7. **Non Jovi (Bon Jovi)**

8. **Earth Wind for Hire (Earth, Wind and Fire)**

9. **Fleetwood Mock (Fleetwood Mac)**

10. **Posin' (Poison)**

11. **Oasisn't (Oasis)**

12. **Nearvana (Nirvana)**

13. **Mandonna (Madonna)**

Numbers 1 and 6 are the microphonies.

Alberta Gotta Do's

DESTROY fondue at the Grizzly House in Banff. Used to be a swinger's club in the '70s, as the table-to-table phones would suggest. So much unusual cubed meat, which you cook to perfection on a 1,000-degree rock at your table.

SHRED Lake Louise on skates. The scenery is inconceivable. Skating outdoors there might be the quintessential Canadian experience. If it's not, having a cocktail in the Chateau Lake Louise afterwards will be.

CARVE fresh pow at Sunshine Village. The slopes are super-sick, as snowboarders who like alliteration would say.

SADDLE UP and slap leather at Rafter Six Ranch, twenty-five kilometres from Canmore. Authentic cowboy experience.

BIRLIN' from Edmonton to Calgary and gettin' a little peckish? Stop in to Old Mexico Taco Buffet in Red Deer.

British Columbia: BC Bahd

Bahd Bands

Michael Bublé

Trooper

The Grapes of Wrath

Econoline Crush

54-40

Skinny Puppy

D.O.A.

The Payolas

Loverboy

Five Notable Bahds

Atom Egoyan. One of Canada's premier film directors. Ever want to feel badly about yourself and the world? Watch *The Sweet Hereafter*.

David Suzuki. Started raising red flags about the environment twenty-five years ago, before it was even part of the public consciousness. Still has abs in his eighties.

Pamela Anderson. Got discovered on the big screen at a BC Lions game. What's more Canadian than that?

Kim Campbell. The first female prime minister in Canadian history!

Rick Hansen. Man in motion! On his world tour, logged more than forty thousand kilometres in thirty-four countries to raise awareness and funds for people with disabilities.

Birlin' to BC

Taggart

I always have a good time in BC. The laid-back attitude in Vancouver is refreshing compared to the rush of Toronto. Between recording and a few relationships, I've spent a couple years there. It's a total bummer when it's raining, so that's why I would find it tough to live there. The Noah's ark vibe once a year takes a toll on the soul, but when it's sunny and fresh, it can't be beat.

I spent a summer travelling Vancouver Island, driving around and pulling over almost anywhere and walking into a river oasis or jumping in a fresh lake. I spent a few days at Sproat Lake near Port Alberni—that place is ridiculous. It's a huge, cross-shaped lake with a crystal-clear view all the way to the treasure trove of logs at its bottom. I'll never forget diving off the dock and feeling like I was in some *Avatar*-level beauty under the water. I'm not a big swimmer, but I am when I'm there. Seeing the Martin Mars water bombers loading up and taking off was a trip too. If you're ever on Vancouver Island, you need to visit that place. It's retirement bait!

Another amazing place is Duncan. I spent a day with the late Cowichan elder Simon Charlie, the legendary Salish master totem carver. He reminded me of Picasso, working tirelessly and with his shirt off. He was all about paying it forward, and it showed in his carving school. His estimated twenty-two truckloads of cedar logs carved is unmatched. He has totems standing in the Royal BC Museum, the Parliament Buildings in Ottawa and other stand-out venues around the world. The man was a true bahd! He was so happy to answer any question, and very eager to give carving tips. I couldn't believe the character in his work. So much depth and personality in the carved faces. You get the feel of his totems and you can pick them out anywhere. Like a true master.

Duncan is an incredible small town. You can feel the connection to the community from the totems on most corners and the friendly folk everywhere. Not to mention the amazing breakfast spots. Cheap too! I went for breakfast at the Arbutus Cafe with four people and it was, like, fifteen bucks all in. So good, bahds.

So there are my moves for Vancouver Island. We all know how awesome Tofino is, but the whole island is full of gems. Get in there!

Vancouver seems to be the place where most people are from somewhere else in Canada. Lots of uprooted bahds. It's interesting how many musicians there are, yet there aren't many clubs to play. More of a party club scene than bands. I used to spend a fair amount of time at the Roxy because you were guaranteed live music. I ripped it up there many times with the local bands, as well as with bahds rolling thru town. Jumping onstage with the fellas from the Trews, playing Band songs, or getting banged up with the *Trailer Park Boys* and Metric. Always a good time at the Roxy.

I loved living in Vancouver while recording OLP's *Gravity* album with Bob Rock. We were in the beautiful studio that Bryan Adams built. Great gear and people there—it was a perfect environment for making music. I spent a lot of nights at Richard's on Richards back then because I was dating a bartender named Cat. She was super-cool, and I would go there after work most nights. So many amazing bands came there—Trail of Dead, Cat Power, Franz Ferdinand, the Walkmen and always the great Nardwuar hanging out, catching all the gold.

I also spent a lot of time at the Commodore Ballroom, one of Canada's finest live venues. That's the place where I felt like we really made it when OLP sold it out in the early days. Amazing sight lines and that incredible floor built on tires so it has give when the crowd gets going. Bouncing up and down with the bands. Fantastic.

The food in Vancouver is well beyond great, home of the best sushi in Tojo's and the most sublime Indian food in Vij's. Indian food is by far my favourite food on Earth, maybe because you can find a good place in almost any city. It's always the safest bet if you're unsure whilst abroad. Nothing sucks more than trying and failing when eating on vacation. There's always a lineup at Vij's because he doesn't take reservations, but it's worth the wait, bahds!

Vantastic

Torrens

 I associate BC with tranquility. Where else can you swim, sail and ski in the same afternoon? Vancouver is pretty and shiny, sprawling and new. The First Nations presence there gives it a depth and soul that's never very far away.

What I really like doing is getting out of the city to explore the coastline. When you grew up near the ocean, water makes you feel at peace, even if it's not the water you grew up around.

The cost of living there is so bananas it creates an interesting cocktail of humans. Old hippies and new money. New buildings, but old trees.

We did a *Jonovision* road show there with headliners Gob. Remember those mafsks? Bunch of punks, in the greatest way.

I have dear friends on Gabriola Island, and it's the kind of place you feel like you could stay blissfully unaware of any problems in the world.

Jason Priestley owns a hotel in Ucluelet. We stayed there when we went to visit my sister-in-law, who was working in Parksville. What a beautiful part of the world that is. Tofino too.

The area has a relaxed gorgeousness, not unlike Jason himself. Hah. First time I met him was at an Anaheim Ducks game. I was there with Mike Smith (Bubbles), and Jason was sitting across the lower bowl with his lovely wife, Naomi.

I was wearing a rugby shirt, and he text-dissed me from all the way across the barn. Something like "Hey, nice to see Torrens is wearing the Duran Duran '80s Collection." Long-range burn via technology. Nice.

After the game they invited us back to their place to have a couple of drinks and chat. The Priestleys are gracious hosts, warm and inviting. Interesting and interested. Little did I know I'd end up working with him just a couple of years later on *Call Me Fitz*, the HBO Canada series shot in Nova Scotia that really showed his range as an actor.

I guess that's what I mean by relaxed. He knows he's Jason Priestley and he knows you know he's Jason Priestley, but he's okay with being him and makes you feel comfortable knowing that. He's also quite a Renaissance man. Great cook, knows a lot about wine, vintage car enthusiast.

You might recall he suffered a terrible car accident during a charity race several years ago. The way he tells it, it was so bad that the

EMTs said, "Well, we might as well make the trip to the hospital to say we did, but there's no way he's going to make it." That might be why he's just so happy to be here, on the planet Earth.

It's not often that you meet people with that kind of profile who are a genuine delight. Jason understands what so very few high-profile actors on a series do: that if a guest star or day player comes on the show and is funny, that makes the show better and him look better in the process.

It takes security to know that. I was supposed to do one day on *Call Me Fitz* in season 1 and I ended up being there all four seasons. It was one of the most fun acting experiences I've ever had because all the actors in the cast were world class and forced you to up your game, like when you're playing tennis against somebody better than you.

And Jason set the fun, respectful tone on set, making everyone else fall in line.

Anyway, if you get a chance, go stay at Terrace Beach Resort. 'Cuz it's beautiful and 'cuz he's a bahd.

The Beachcombers

Torrens

When I was twelve I went to visit the set of *The Beachcombers* and was shocked to discover that the pie in Molly's Reach was plastic. And that the restaurant only had three walls. And that Relic's shed just housed a bunch of old ropes—the interiors were shot elsewhere. How could this be? The characters on this show, from Bruno Gerussi's Nick to Jackson Davies's Mountie, were so real, so believable and *so* Canadian, it was hard to accept that they were fictitious. All except Relic, who I still believe is real.

Bahd Ambassador
Rikki F.

TnT resident episode cataloguer Rikki lives in BC and sent these our way when we asked for her suggestions. Talk about going a-bahd and beyond!

- **Blue Moose, 322 Wallace Street, Hope.** This well-known local pit stop is an epic haven for coffee lovers, transients, local artists and live jazz musicians alike. The colourful moose-laden environment is spacious, yet cozy, and the food is freshly made in house. Overall atmosphere is friendly, diverse, delicious—much like Canada.
- **Yellow Deli, 45859 Yale Road, Chilliwack.** Sandwiches, hearty soups/chili made daily in house, and incredible juices. The tiny shack has the feel of a log cabin, with massive slabs of tree trunks for tables. Perfect for starting off on a road trip, after a long shift at work, or just sheer curiosity towards the intriguing commune-esque backstory of the Yellow Deli.
- **Hilltop Diner, 23904 Fraser Highway, Langley.** This gem first opened for business in the '40s to service a roadside motel on the same property. Since then, not much has changed. The greasy dive is well known for its phenomenal in-house pies, homely decor and foot-tall burger.
- **Honey Doughnuts & Goodies, 4373 Gallant Ave., North Vancouver.** Tucked away in Deep Cove, this doughnut shop has

a constant lineup out the door and is well known for its calorie-filled, homemade doughnuts delivered warm and powdery to your piehole.

- **Tomahawk, 1550 Philip Avenue, North Vancouver.** The original Tomahawk opened in the '20s, oftentimes trading meals for First Nations artwork and artifacts. This breakfast joint is a staple for any foodie. The atmosphere highlights the history of the First Nations peoples in the Capilano area and serves up some of the tastiest, greasiest grub you'll find.

- **Anton's Pasta Bar, 4260 East Hastings Street, Burnaby.** Anyone who's anyone has crammed carbs into their gut at Anton's. This family-friendly restaurant is known for its massive servings, its ninety-minute lineups out the door and for presenting a pen to any patron who finishes their meal.

- **FreeWheelin' Records, 33707 Essendene Avenue, Abbotsford.** This mom-and-pop record store is completely classic Canadianity. Owned by a couple in their sixties who work side by side with their massive dog, this is a staple for anyone interested in new or used vinyl. They also carry a variety of music-related biographies and books, as well as glass art. Wifey keeps a notebook with handwritten records of each sale, with your name so they can greet customers by first name and recollect their musical tastes/preferences.

- **Krazy Bob's Music Emporium, 20484 Fraser Highway, Langley.** Krazy Bob lives up to his name through his inability to spell, to say no to any potential merchandise for his floor-to-ceiling-stocked store and to engage in verbal banter with customers—poking fun and crossing the line without fail. He is one of the strangest characters you'll ever meet, yet is brilliant at the same time. From VHS to vinyl to cassettes to CDs to random figurines, games, books and iconic pop-culture gems, Bob's hoard-fest is a must-see paradise for music lovers.

- **Stawamus Chief, Squamish.** Unquestionably, one of the best hikes in BC. This seven-kilometre quad-breaker essentially takes you straight up, utilizing ladders, chains and the natural landscape to bring hikers atop three separate peaks, overlooking the provincial park, the community of Squamish, Mount Garibaldi, the Pacific Ocean and dozens of surrounding islands.

The Price of Friendship

Torrens

Sometimes when you meet high-profile media types, it's a disappointment. There's no way they can measure up to the high hopes you have for them.

Shelagh Rogers of CBC Radio fame is not one of those people. Somehow warmer in person than she sounds on the radio, she is funnier than you'd ever imagine and even, on occasion, a little bit saucy. When she is, it's thrilling.

The strange thing is she sometimes took heat from the public for being phony. Or *sounding* it on the radio anyway. No one could possibly be that warm, folks would say. She's too gushy, they would say. Boy, are they wrong. She actually is that warm, that kind, that gushy. It's like her every nerve ending is open to experience. She actually does feel every little thing and cares that deeply about people.

Which, for my money, makes this story that much better.

I've never really felt like part of the establishment, such as it is in Canadian show business. It might be because of geography. The

East Coast is such a remote part of the country that we feel disassociated from what goes on in the rest of Canada.

It sounds a bit crazy, but there actually is an adjustment period whenever I leave the safe refuge of the sticks for the bright lights. It might be because I didn't grow up that way, with the flash, dash and cash. Still, the odd time I find myself in big, strange rooms with fancy folks and wonder how I got there.

One such evening was a benefit for the *Walrus* magazine a few years ago. Don't get me wrong—super-nice people, just not my typical weeknight event. My dear friend Jenny had an extra ticket, and I really enjoy her company. We knew our mutual friend Shelagh would be there and we wanted to support her.

The event was a silent auction of messages in a bottle, with handwritten notes donated by everyone from Desmond Tutu to Bill Clinton. Cool.

There was only one live auction item, and it was a dandy: five predictions for the future, handwritten by Margaret Atwood, in a crystal decanter. The live auction was emceed by the aforementioned and adored Shelagh Rogers.

The room was fancy and loud. Some Big Bank types were rubbing elbows with some Seamus O'Regans and Stuart McLeans and such. Because the room was unwieldy to begin with and L-shaped to boot, Shelagh invited Albert Schultz of *Street Legal*, *Side Effects* and Soulpepper Theatre Company fame (note: he only does things that start with the letter *s*) and me to be the spotters as the bids flew in.

Only problem was, they didn't. People were tipsy and chatty and it was hard to track what was going on.

The bid got up to somewhere around $3,000, and poor Shelagh

was trying everything in her power to drive it up. What seemed like several minutes passed, with the bidding stalled.

Sitting by the side of the stage, Margaret Atwood herself offered to throw in lunch with the winner. Solid incentive for Atwood fans.

That drove the bid up to $5,000, where it stalled again. In the semi-silence, I stage-whispered to Albert, "We should split it for $5,000 and take Atwood to Subway, 'cuz that would be funny." He chuckled but didn't bite.

I've been in that position as a host before, and Shelagh is far better and more experienced than me. She was no doubt waiting for something, anything, to move things along so she could wrap it up.

She had heard what I'd said to Albert behind her back and said into the mic, "Jonathan has offered to split it with someone—right, Jonathan?"

I was a little drunk. All eyes were on me. I didn't feel I could renege. So I smiled and nodded.

Rebecca Eckler, a reporter from the *National Post,* sitting near the front, agreed to split it for $7,000, and the next thing I knew Shelagh was saying, "Sold to Rebecca and Jonathan for $7,000."

Seven *thousand* dollars. Meaning my half was $3,500.

I couldn't even remember what I'd "won" until Rebecca approached me afterwards and said that she'd read Margaret Atwood to her daughter in the womb when she was pregnant and would really love to have the handwritten predictions. But I could have the decanter.

And I could take Margaret Atwood to lunch. Which, to this day, I still never have, but should. It would be fun. There's someone else whose reputation I'll bet is far removed from who she actually is. Sources say she's deadly funny.

Not sure whatever happened to the crystal decanter either, but Shelagh is still a great friend, and you can't put a price on that.

Oh, wait—yes, you can. It's $3,500.

British Columbia Gotta Do's

HOOVER a Happy Tuna sushi roll at Blue Ginger in Nanaimo.

BANG OUT a pedicure with cocktails at Tigh-Na-Mara Seaside Spa Resort in Parksville.

BUTCHER a scone or croissant at Bodhi's in Nanaimo.

PUMMEL a chocolate ganache brownie at Cascadia Bakery in Victoria.

ANNIHILATE a hike at Pinnacles Provincial Park in Quesnel.

Newfoundland and Labrador: Day Boilers and Alan Doylers

Bahd Bands

So many!

Great Big Sea

Fortunate Ones

The Once

The Ennis Sisters

Hey Rosetta!

The Irish Descendants

Thomas Trio and the Red Albino

Rawlins Cross

Figgy Duff

Repartee

Ron Hynes

Colleen Power

The Dardanelles

Five Notable Bahds

For some reason, narrowing it down to just five is especially hard in Newfoundland and Labrador. Fortunately, Rick Mercer, Gordon Pinsent and the *Codco/22 Minutes* crowd are covered elsewhere in this book.

Andy Jones. Stole the movie *Rare Birds* out from under William Hurt. Brother to Cathy (of *22 Minutes* fame) and father to Codco,

Andy is one of Canada's all-time best and most committed comedic performers. That he's so selective about what he does makes him that much more intriguing.

Ed Riche. Ed has written many funny books, but *Rare Birds* is arguably the funniest. So funny, it was turned into a movie starring William Hurt and Andy Jones!

Joey Smallwood. Brought Newfoundland into Canada in 1949. Perhaps a divisive character in Newfoundland and Labrador, but his accomplishments are hard to argue with.

Bob Cole. *The* voice of *Hockey Night in Canada.* "Oh baby."

Seamus O'Regan. From *Canada AM* to Canadian MP.

Bonus Bahd

Shannon Tweed! Synonymous with erotic thrillers. Married some guy with a really long tongue.

Give 'Er

Torrens

This is my favourite fact about the Rock, and it tells you everything you need to know: Newfoundlanders make the lowest average income per capita in Canada but give the most to charity. Doesn't that say a lot about a group of humans?

Speaking of clich-ehs being at least partly true, the ones that say Newfoundlanders are warm and funny and love to party? Those are certainly true.

Not too long ago, the Yuk Yuk's comedy club in St. John's closed down. I was talking to Steve Dylan, a standup comic and turbo-bahd.

His feeling was it might not have lasted because it's the only club in the country where the hecklers are almost always funnier than whoever's onstage. Usually, seasoned comics get pretty good at the art of the shutdown, but Steve said that in that club, you'd often have to stop and acknowledge that the heckle was actually hilarious.

Crushin' the Rock

Taggart

The first time I arrived on the rock, I felt like I was at a family reunion. Like I was with my Dad's Glaswegian clan. Everyone talks to you like they knew you already, or they don't care who you are and you better be noice! There's an air of "Try to be cool and fit in, or fuck off!" I love the slight harshness and the way they use local slang even though they know you haven't a clue what it means.

My first cab ride from the airport was classic. I had to ask so many questions just to understand what the driver was saying. The amount of creativity in each slang word was mind-boggling. I was blown away. You gotta keep your ears peeled!

One time I was with some good friends from the Bally Haly golf club in St. John's, Jason Hill and Andy George, two prime examples of how great the people from St. John's are. We were playing golf in the early afternoon and having drinks. Little did I know that I was having myself a "day boiler." I asked them what the hell that meant, and they told me it's when you get banged up during the day. Try to tell me that's not the most classic phrase for that circumstance, ever!

Even the bigwigs in St. John's have big hearts. I was playing the Mile One Centre with OLP in the late '90s and it was a great show, packed and all that stuff. We met Alan Doyle and the other boys from Great Big Sea, and they invited us to an after-party they had arranged. We went to the club that they had closed for the party, and we walked in to see the most lobster on ice we've ever seen. What a great night we had, crushing lobster, getting banged up and kissing cods.

What a beautiful place. Everyone knows everyone like it's a small town, and if you give respect, you get respected. "Take it as you see it" seems to be the underlying motto there. Too big for your britches? You probably won't like it there, real quick. Anyone I know who suffers from ego trips can't stand the place. A quick and easy way to find out if someone is worth any salt is if they've been to St. John's and loved it. If they didn't, you know that you can drop them like a hot rock.

I played the Salmon Festival in Grand Falls a couple times with OLP. The first time, we had to wait forever to play because Dr. Hook was super-late. We went on at, like, 1 a.m. Whatev-salad, it was still a gas. Another time we played with the local and great Hey Rosetta!, one of my favourite Canadian bands, as well as Akon, the rapper. Funny story: Akon was pissed off because he'd played Detroit the night before, and because Grand Falls is linked with Windsor, Newfoundland, he thought they were playing in Windsor, Ontario—hahaha! Imagine what he thought when they were heading to the airport instead of making a quick run across the bridge or tunnel into Canada. Not to mention the three-hour drive from Gander. So funny. He played a fantastic show anyway. The crowd went crazy for him.

REALtor or FAKEtor

The weirdest free-giveaway ad we ever saw was on Craigslist in LA. A woman was giving away avocados from the tree in her backyard to anyone over five feet, six inches tall.

She'd picked all the ones she could reach.

Guess from the following Kijiji ads which ones were really up for grabs for *nada*!

1. **Labrador City: Free fifteen-by-twenty-foot free-standing pressure-treated deck**
2. **Gander: Free hugs**
3. **St. John's: Covered litter box for cat**
4. **Stephenville: Sixteen feet of Sonotube, six inches around**
5. **St. John's: Small amount of rhubarb**

Only number 2 is fake. The rest were actual ads.

Some Day on Clothes, B'y

Torrens

Several years ago, I shot a movie in St. John's. It was a cute little indie feature called *The Bread Maker*, written by my hugely talented and funny friend Sherry White.

I should've known I was in for a unique experience when, as the plane was preparing to land, the captain came on the intercom and said, "Ladies and gentlemen, it's a windy one down there, which will make landing a bit of an adventure. *But*, we'll take a crack at 'er."

"Take a crack at 'er"? That was not confidence-instilling at all.

The colourful language of Newfoundland and Labrador has been well documented, and I got my first taste of it the moment I sat in the back seat of a cab from the airport. The driver, wearing a cap straight outta *Newsies*, turned around and said, "Some day on clothes, b'y."

I really wanted to know what he meant, but I just didn't.

Turns out "some day on clothes" is what you say on a windy day, meaning it's a good time to hang your wash out on the clothesline.

On the other hand, if it's too windy, you replay with "Naw, b'y, it's a wraparound." 'Cuz it's so windy your clothes will wrap around the line.

I loved my time in St. John's. The production rented me a spot on Battery Road on the way to Signal Hill. It's easy to put on a lot of miles walking around that town. The scenery is so spectacular, you almost don't notice the hills. Almost.

On a couple of weekends, I rented a car and just drove. It's easy to fall in love with the place. It has such natural charm and character—like your grandpa's cardigan with elbow patches and a Werther's in the pocket.

My favourite destination was an inn called the Fishers' Loft, in Port Rexton, out near Trinity. World-class food, views and rooms. At that time, the Fishers' three-legged dog would guide you on hikes out around the beaches and cliffs. The Fishers' Loft has since been taken over by Luke Fisher, whom I've known for a long time. He was an assistant director on films around Halifax and played the fiddle in bands too. He and his partner Molly Sexton moved back when they had a baby, and now he and his brother run the inn.

Which brings up a good point about people from Newfoundland. When I was working on *The Bread Maker*, the crew was borderline intimidating because no one excelled in just one artistic arena. The costume designer also played in a band. The assistant director was also a painter. The props folks were also dancers. And on the weekends, they would take turns volunteering to work at each other's shows. Artists in the truest sense because they stayed in the place they loved and made art for art's sake. Isolation breeds collaboration. It was inspiring to witness and even be a part of for that brief time.

Bahd Ambassadors
Fortunate Ones

Andrew and Cat are a duo in music and in life. And they're totally adora-bahds. If you haven't, you should buy their Christmas album. They take on Kenny and Dolly's "Christmas without You" and *win!* Here are their tips for N & L.

- **Adelaide Oyster House** has created, perhaps, the world's greatest fish taco. It consists of a beer-battered portion of the mighty Atlantic codfish, smothered in fiery adobo sauce (great for a cold night in Sin Jawn's), a sprinkling of purple cabbage, jalapeno, thinly sliced radish and cilantro. Spritz a bit of fresh lime juice on there—friggin' wicked. They also have a deadly cocktail called the El Camino, which has tequila, cilantro, jalapeno, homemade citrus bar mix and margarita salt. Sweet and spicy. Amazing staff, good music and a great atmosphere, Adelaide is a must-go while visiting the capital city.

- **Bonavista Social Club** is a small, family-run restaurant in Upper Amherst Cove. Before you enter the restaurant, which was designed and built by the owner's master carpenter father, you'll be taken by the stunning view—rolling hills, a vast bay, incredible sunsets and a scattered whale. The BSC has a large, home-grown organic garden that provides all the produce found in the menu items. The chefs also use meat, milk and cheese from animals that live, free range, on the premises. The menu is small and perfectly refined. You'll find moose ragout on hand-rolled pasta, wood-fired pizza, fresh fish, warm bread with salt and rosemary butter and delicious rhubarb lemonade. The moose burger is unreal and you'll have trouble not pounding several. Exceptional service, beautiful scenery and amazing food make the Bonavista Social Club a must on any trip down the Bonavista highway.

- **Skerwink Trail** in Port Rexton is one of our favourite hikes in the province. It is a hilly 5K that takes you along a stunning portion of the coast of Trinity Bay. Plunging cliffs and incredible scenery define the trail, and on a good day you'll see lots of whales and sea birds. After the hike, make your way to the new Port Rexton Brewing Company. They're quickly becoming mythic in Newfoundland for creating some of the province's finest craft beer. Be sure to try the IPA and the porter. Bring a DD. It'd be a sin not to crush several of their frosty soldiers.

You Can't Outcharm the Codfather

Torrens

For the CBC's fiftieth anniversary, I was honoured to be one of very few Ceeb-lebrities™ who were chosen to greet Her Majesty when she visited the Broadcast Centre for a very special eighteen-minute period to mark this auspicious occasion.

Gordon Pinsent was chosen. Rick Mercer too.

To say we had to go to Queen school is a bit of an overstatement, but we certainly had to learn specific royal protocol in the weeks leading up to the visit. Don't hold out your hand to shake unless she does, don't speak unless spoken to, don't call her Liz, don't put your hand on the small of the Queen's back (as a premier did once). Things that should be fairly obvious but bear repeating.

I happen to have it on good authority from a police friend of mine who's detailed Her Maj before that she has a great sense of humour and loves to keep those closest to her on their toes. One story he told me involved her motorcade suddenly and unexpectedly exiting the highway because, as they later found out, Liz wanted french fries from a drive-thru.

She apparently totally "gets" that she's the Queen and, in typical British fashion, is quite self-deprecating. I love that.

So I passed Queen school with flying colours and the words of the organizers ringing in my ears: *Don't stray from the script. DON'T.*

My script was quite formal, as you might expect. It dovetailed out of Gordon Pinsent's line before me and I had it properly memorized: "Your Majesty, the CBC is also a place to laugh. For five decades now, Canadians from coast to coast to coast have made this their destination . . . *blah, blah, blah.*"

To be honest, I hadn't really given much thought to how cool this was. I'd been busy travelling back and forth to LA and guest-hosting *This Hour Has 22 Minutes*.

On the episode of 22 that had aired the night before, I had done a Linden MacIntyre impression, wherein the *Fifth Estate* journalist was investigating his own soul. It was kind of niche-y, but my "Linden lilt" is pretty good, if I do say so myself. His wife, Carol Off, agrees and she even interviewed me about it on *As It Happens*.

The reason Linden is relevant: there I was, standing on Queen Row as Her Majesty approached. I suddenly got very nervous as Gordon Pinsent charmed the crown right off her. With his gravelly voice and twinkly eyes, she was laughing like a schoolgirl.

I felt butterflies in my stomach and my mouth went dry as she was guided over to me. "That's the *Queen*," I thought.

As I was being introduced, I licked my lips while looking directly in her eyes. "This is Jonathan Torrens, he's an actor and producer here."

The Queen said, "Oh, you're a producer, are you?"

All I could think was *Stick to the script. Stick to the script.* How was I supposed to get from what she said to what I was supposed to say?

I looked around to collect my thoughts and made direct eye contact with *Linden MacIntyre* over the Queen's shoulder. He gave me the "I'm watching you" eyes, as a joke. Or was it? Had he seen last night's *22*? Was he offended? I thought, *I'll have to find him later and take his temperature on it. Right now, I'd better say something to the Queen of England.*

"Yeah, yeah. But Your Majesty, the CBC is also a place to laugh . . ."

I *yeah-yeah*'d the Queen. All the girlish Gordonness evaporated and I stumbled through the rest of my spiel. Then she was gone. To Rick Mercer. Who also reduced her to clotted cream in his hands.

As I was taking a deep breath, suddenly Prince Philip was in my face.

"What do you do here?" he asked.

"Oh, I work in kids TV."

"Is that you there?" he pointed over my shoulder.

I turned around to see a Muppet from *Sesame Park* (the Canadian version of *Sesame Street*) on display. When I turned back around to explain, he was gone.

Getting dissed by Prince Philip was, oddly enough, my highlight of the night.

One of my favourite Gordon Pinsent stories comes from when they were shooting *The Shipping News* in Newfoundland. Kevin Spacey was the star, and he brought half a dozen security guards with him from LA.

They realized quite quickly that he wouldn't need much security because Newfoundlanders couldn't give a frozen cod tongue who he was. So they sent most of the guards back to California, but erected some concrete girders to keep the crowd back instead.

A few days in they realized that the girders wouldn't be necessary for this well-behaved crowd either, so they removed them. So the story goes, a stampede of locals ran right past Kevin Spacey and swarmed Gordon Pinsent to tell him how they might be related. "Now, your cousin is my wife's great-aunt."

Gordon was also apparently a little hard to find from time to time. On a movie that size, it takes a while to set up the shots. More than once when they were finally ready to go, Mr. Pinsent was nowhere to be found.

Turns out he would be in a neighbourhood kitchen, having a visit and game of crib over tea.

Gordon Pinsent. What a GD legend.

Mike Stevens: A Bahddist Monk

Torrens

This story takes place in Labrador, but it'll take me a little bit to get there. Polar bear with me. It's worth the journey.

There is a core group of us that travels north for the Peter Gzowski golf tournaments for literacy. Too many to mention, impossible to forget. Some of Canada's best singers, poets and authors have donated their time to this great cause over the years. But one in particular embodies the spirit of Canadianity better than anyone I've ever met.

His name is Mike Stevens and he's the best harmonica player in the world.

If you listen to TnT, you might recall we named Mike our Bahd of the Week on an early episode. His incredible and inspiring story goes something like this.

He's from Sarnia, Ontario, and worked in a petrochemical plant there in his twenties. His secret passion was playing harmonica, though, so on weekends he'd slip across the border and play in blues clubs. What he really wanted to do for a living was play bluegrass harmonica—an even rarer goal.

When he started playing bluegrass, some audience members would turn their backs on him because harmonica isn't a traditional bluegrass instrument. But his talent was undeniable. Even to hardcore heavies like Jim and Jesse McReynolds, who struck a deal with Mike. They couldn't put him officially on the bill because their core fans would protest. What they were willing to do, however, was start playing "Orange Blossom Special" every night and then stop, saying that what the tune could really use is a harmonica. Planted in the crowd, Mike would hop up, burn the place down and they'd pass the hat for him.

He was soon making more this way than Jim and Jesse were. His goal was to become the best player in the world and he was well on his way. He's played the Grand Ole Opry more than four hundred times. He was in Dwight Yoakam's band. Things were really happening for him.

On a tour stop in Happy Valley-Goose Bay, Labrador, in 2000, Mike picked up a local paper before the gig and read a story about kids sniffing gas in nearby Sheshatshiu. At the concert that night, he dedicated "Amazing Grace" to those kids and felt a tension come over the audience. Clearly, he'd hit a nerve by mentioning the story.

After the gig, a local reporter approached him and told Mike he was from Sheshatshiu and would be happy to drive him out there the next morning so he could see firsthand how devastating this problem was. Mike agreed, and the next morning he found himself bombing down a rough gravel road on the way to a place that no longer felt like it could be in first-world Canada.

As they arrived in the town, the reporter pointed out a group of eight to ten kids sniffing gas and slammed on the brakes. He told Mike to get out and do something.

So Mike did the only thing he could think to do. He played the harmonica for them.

At first they laughed at him, and then with him, and soon they were putting down the gas and asking him questions about his own life. He in turn asked questions about theirs. They were really connecting.

In that moment, he realized the very reason he plays music.

Back on tour, the next day the band arrived in Alert, Nunavut. A military official told Mike there was a phone call for him. It was *As It Happens*, the CBC radio show. Someone had videotaped Mike's encounter and it had made the news. *AIH* wanted to hear the story from his perspective.

Mike let it all hang out on air. He was still rattled, in shock and disgusted that people could live in these conditions in this country, and he was going to find a way to help. Seeing as how music seemed to really resonate with them, Mike suggested that if people had old instruments they wanted to donate, he'd find a way to deliver them.

People responded to Mike and to the story. Soon he needed a transport truck to get the instruments up there.

He started playing fewer gigs and using much of the money he did make to buy harmonicas to hand out to kids. As he put it, the kids who are in school aren't the ones who need the attention. It's the ones out in the woods late at night, sniffing gas, and with no desire to live, who need help. So those are the ones he seeks out.

For years, at his own expense and at great risk to his health, he's made trips to some of the hardest places in the North, to share his gift of music and compassion. He founded a not-for-profit called ArtsCan Circle, devoted to spreading the music, instruments and hope throughout the North. He hand-selects musicians to go into communities, unpaid, to teach kids how to play.

The program is in its second generation. Kids are using donated recording equipment to make albums for their bands and also to record stories by their elders in languages that are slipping away.

Now, ArtsCan Circle is in more than a dozen communities, and Mike has personally bought and handed out more than twenty thousand harmonicas.

That, to me, is the very definition of Canadianity. I actually produced a documentary about Mike called *A Walk in My Dream*. If you ever want to watch it, I'll loan you the DVD. No late fees or anything!

In the spring of 2016, I was honoured to present Mike with the Slaight Music Humanitarian Award at the Canadian Country Music Awards. It was so much fun watching him try—naturally—to deflect all the compliments and love coming his way.

Newfoundland Gotta Do's

TREK to Fogo Island Inn. We'll be honest, we haven't been there ourselves yet, but it's on da bucket list. Pictures look incredible and first-hand reports are out of this world.

DESTROY dinner at Mallard Cottage. Alan Doyle's brudder-in-law is the chef. It's set in Quidi Vidi Gut, the most "You've gotta be kidding me, this is real?" of locations. Food is local, fresh and off-the-chain creative.

CRUSH some cod tongues at Tavola. In keeping with the Great Big Sea theme, multi-instrumentalist Bob Hallett owns this joint. Small plates and tapas, but fried chicken too. They'll serve whatever's fresh any given night.

DROP IN to the Woody Point writers' festival. Our homie and CBC legend Shelagh Rogers is a staple at this event, which pairs live readings from famous Canadian authors (Lawrence Hill, Michael Crummey) with live performances by Canadian musicians (Ron Sexsmith, Stephen Fearing, Amelia Curran).

BIRL into the Burl Gathering. *This Hour Has 22 Minutes* host Shaun Majumder has started an annual event in his tiny hometown of Burlington (population 350-ish). It combines good food with good times and great hangs in a remote location.

SHOVE OFF to Dildo. Yes, there's a town in Newfoundland called Dildo. Years ago, there was a movement afoot to change the name because it might be offensive to some. The townsfolk rallied and shot back, "We were called Dildo before that other thing . . . change the name of *it!*"

The North: A Tundra of Fundra!

Five Notable Bands

Ethel Blondin-Andrew. First Aboriginal woman elected to the Canadian Parliament.

Godson. For the longest time, Godson held the distinction of being the only rapper in northern Canada. Solid flow, solid guy. J-Roc actually appeared in his video for "Like This/It's Over."

Jordin Tootoo. Born in Manitoba, but the North can claim him as its own. NHLer and, more important, role model to young hockey players from all over the North.

Nellie Cournoyea. Sixth premier of the Northwest Territories. She is known and adored everywhere you go in NWT.

Tanya Tagaq. A throat singer from Cambridge Bay who's taken her traditional sounds, stories and songs to the masses.

Whitehorse, Yellowknife and Whatchamiqaluit

Torrens

For twenty years, I've been travelling up north for the annual Peter Gzowski Invitational Golf Tournament for Literacy. It's truly a privilege to get to see parts of Canada that so few people ever get to.

I'm genuinely interested in seeing how people live in different parts of the country. I've gotten to drive dogsleds, eat muktuk (whale blubber!) and see how traditional prints are made. One of the most profound experiences of my life was lying on a deck in Yellowknife in the middle of winter, looking up at the northern lights, listening to a nine-year-old confess that she was worried her grandparents' traditional language was fading away. It's a magical, spiritual, haunting, devastating, gorgeous place.

Plus, as a Canadian, I feel so much pride that this breathtaking lunar landscape is part of our country too. You don't even realize how you take trees for granted until you're up above the tree line. Imagine the price of wood in a place with no trees. The cost of a tomato or lettuce that had to be flown in. Everything is at a premium because of shipping costs.

The trade-off is spectacular, though. Caribou steaks, Arctic char, muskox jerky. Plus, drive fifteen minutes out of any town and you're in the wilderness. Not like "go for a stroll in Tilley hats on a nicely groomed trail" wilderness, more like "there might be a wolverine around so we should be careful" wilderness. For a "southerner" like me, it can be equal parts exhilarating and terrifying.

The northern lights will make you believe in a higher power. Maybe that's why Inuit people are so spiritual.

We shot two episodes of *Street Cents* in Iqaluit all those years ago. The only thing I really remember is a parody called *Hudson Baywatch*.

The first time I went to Yellowknife was in 1992 for Caribou Carnival, and I was immediately captivated by the people and the place. Yes, it's cold, but it just makes you that much more thankful for the sun when it does shine.

In many ways, Yellowknife is like any other city. It's got hustle and bustle, busy professionals running to meetings, organized chaos. But it's also got a unique heartbeat. The population is transient, to a degree. Some folks are just there on short work or study terms, and some people are just passing through on their way to far more remote places to work or hunt.

You meet a curious assortment of southerners up there. Some moved up just because they love the outdoor lifestyle. Others, you can tell, are on the run from something or someone. Still others need to make money fast. Time and time again, you hear the same story about people who came up for a week in 1986 and never left. Or left but just couldn't get it out of their system and had to come back.

You also hear the stories about people taking jobs up there, getting off the plane and getting right back on it. It's not for everybody, but those who do like it, love it.

There are real opportunities in Canada's North for those who are ambitious, adventurous and spirited enough. I remember going to a dinner party on that first trip to Yellowknife with a bunch of people in their early twenties, and they all seemed so *together*. So-and-so was the manager of recreation for the city, so-and-so was the deputy mayor. The region seems to attract people who are wise and accomplished beyond their years.

If you're ambitious or motivated, you can write your own ticket. Good pay, isolation benefits. There's a lot to like about life in the North aside from how spectacularly beautiful it is.

Those who are from there know this and take great pride in the geography that surrounds them.

One night at a house party in Holman, I was introduced to a First Nations guy who was going polar bear hunting the next day with a bow and arrow. You can imagine how jazzed the interviewer in me was to learn this. I couldn't help myself.

"Are you scared?"

"How do you find them?"

"What if you miss?"

"Do you get a second shot?"

"How do you get it home?"

"Why go alone?"

"What will you eat?"

"What will you wear?"

He was politely indulging my questions but wasn't really engaged. I could tell that something was bothering him about my outrageous level of interest. Finally, the guy who had introduced us pulled me aside and told me that in his culture, you never talk about a hunt beforehand, out of respect for the animal.

Whoa. Cool. Respect for the animal you're hunting.

The relationship between animals and people in the North is a special one. They coexist and are codependent, almost like they respect each other's ability to survive in that harsh climate.

Schools encourage families to take their kids out of class for a couple of weeks and go live "on the land," fishing and hunting, learning traditional survival methods. Schools embrace the culture as part of a child's education. I just love that the surroundings up there inform every aspect of a person's existence. What they eat. What they wear. When they sleep.

The first time I went to Whitehorse was for a Gzowski tournament in the summer, when there's almost twenty-four hours of daylight. This poses a whole different series of challenges than when there's round-the-clock darkness. Your body doesn't want to sleep when the sun is shining. You need blackout curtains. You come out of the bar at closing time and there are kids running around, playing tag. It doesn't make sense to you, but their parents figure they'll sleep when they're tired.

There are three cities in North America where I've instantly thought, upon arriving there, "I could live here, no problem." One is Chicago. One is San Francisco. The other is Whitehorse.

It's the best of all worlds. It's clean yet cosmopolitan. There are a lot of outdoor activities, but there's also a huge arts scene. There's work and fun to be had.

There's even a Starbucks.

One afternoon, at the suggestion of the owner of the hotel where I was staying, I rented a car and drove from Whitehorse to Skagway, Alaska. Me, the open road and some *Gord's Gold* blasting out the windows of my Ford Explorer. I'd be lying if I said there weren't moments when it was hard to see the road because of the tears in my eyes. The majestic mountains, Gord, the open road, my love of this country . . . it was almost too much Canadianity to bear.

Speaking of bears, I spotted a couple on the side of the road and slowed to take a picture. Several other cars had pulled over too.

The bears seemed oblivious. They were just basking in the afternoon sun.

I rolled my window down to snap a quick picture, and the guy in the car behind me got out and came flying up to my window.

"What the hell are you doing, man? Do you know how fast a bear can run? Put your window up. That thing will be over here and in your car before you know it!"

All I could think was "Then I guess you'd better get back in *yours*, bahd."

You pass the world's tiniest desert on that drive, near the village of Carcross. It's about the size of a Ford Festiva. The world is full of wonders, eh, bahds?

Aside from the cities, these northern Gzowski trips have taken us to small towns with intriguing names like Rankin Inlet, Cambridge Bay, Hay River, Holman and Inuvik. Part of what we do on these literacy trips is visit schools and daycare centres, seniors residences and shop classes. We divide and conquer, sharing what we know. In my case it's a bit weird, because I'm not known as a singer/songwriter. I'm not a poet. I'm not a standup.

Ever notice how, in the country, everyone barters. He fixes your vehicle, you do his plumbing. She does your electrical, you do her painting.

I have no skills to barter.

So when I go to schools, we rap. "I'm not a rapper, but I play one on TV" is how it starts. Then I tell them that Dr. Seuss was the first rapper in history. Then I do a couple of J-Roc verses and try to bleep the swears. Then I get them to write and perform rap songs about what they know.

Sometimes they work in groups, sometimes alone. Sometimes

their raps are about polar bears or hockey, sometimes about suicide and how painful it is to lose a loved one.

There have been moments that make my heart explode and others that leave me feeling crushed. There is a depth to northern souls, and you can see it in their eyes.

One moment in particular, fifteen or so years ago, I was at a school in Rae-Edzo, outside Yellowknife, a community that's now called Behchoko.

It's a school where the population fluctuates depending on the weather. When it's very cold outside, there could be four hundred kids there. They come because it's warm. When the weather is nice, there might be forty kids there. The rest are off hunting and fishing and occasionally getting into mischief.

On this particular day, I was there to talk up literacy on behalf of my broadcasting idol, Peter Gzowski. It was going okay. We were discussing favourite books and why reading is important. As usual, the ones up front were attentive and participating. The ones in back were joking around and restless.

So on a whim, I asked a kid in the back row why reading is important. He was a class-clown type who had chirped me a couple of times. Quite well, I might add.

He rolled his eyes at my question, then paused for a moment and said, "Because reading can take me places I can't go in my room."

Kaboom. The entire gym burst into applause and Mr. Mouthy was beaming with pride. I'll never forget it.

A few years back, Barney Bentall, Russell deCarle from Prairie Oyster and I visited a jail in Iqaluit. Most of the inmates are good dudes who made a couple of bad decisions. In some cases, they'd commit a serious enough crime in the fall to get a sentence to last the winter, which is both heartbreaking and shrewd—a warm place to stay with three square meals a day. Genius.

Since, as I've mentioned, I lack an actual trade, I mostly stand at the back of the room and watch these musical monsters share their enormous gifts with delighted audiences. Barney and Russell are warm, magnetic cats.

I was watching them play the Johnny Cash song "Ring of Fire" when an inmate approached me and asked if I wanted to do a bump with him in the bathroom. I'm a little slow on the draw and more naive than you might expect, so I honestly thought he meant some kind of exercise.

"No, a *bump*. Like, *cocaine*."

"Uh, aren't we in a jail?"

"Yeah, but it's totally cool."

I explained that I don't do cocaine. If there's one thing I don't need, it's something to make me "even more me." There's a big history of addiction in my family and I can't even eat Werther's in moderation, so the last thing I need is to "try" cocaine. Took me long enough to kick a two-pack-a-day Mentos habit.

"Oh, thanks anyway, but I'm good." I tried to change the subject. "What are you up to today?"

He told me his plan was to watch me give him cigarettes. I didn't have any, so offered the only thing I had on me. Gum.

"You want a piece of gum?"

His eyes widened. He and his friend exchanged glances. Yes, he said. He'd *love* a piece of gum. His friend said he'd love one too.

So I gave them each a piece of gum. I think it was Dentyne Cinna-mint, or some other clumsy portmanteau. It was a nice moment. They thanked me repeatedly. It's nothing, I assured them.

Moments later, in the processing cell between the outside and the inside, we were gathering our stuff when a guard came flying into the room. "Did one of you guys give an inmate gum?"

Everyone looked around at each other and shook their heads no. Who would've done such a thing?

I could feel my face turning red, but I slowly put my hand up and confessed what I'd done. Sheepishly, I asked why this was such a bad thing (especially considering what his first suggestion was).

They can use it to jam the locks. It's contraband.

I then had to confess that I'd given it to his friend as well. He asked me to describe them, and I started bumbling out that they were both wearing grey sweatpants and navy blue T-shirts. Like the entire prison population was. That's their uniform.

Oops.

Of all the places I've been lucky enough to go in the North, there's one that holds a special place in my heart: Pangnirtung. It might be because the approach on a plane is so memorable. The plane's wing tips barely miss scraping the magnificent peaks on either side of the gravel runway. Stark, white, snow-capped mountains entirely surround this happy hamlet.

The people are friendly, happy and productive. The print shop in Pang is known all over the world, so morale is high.

The lineup for this trip boasted some heavy Canadianity: Strombo was there for MuchMusic, Kim D'Eon from *Street Cents* and one of the Moffatts. Remember them? "Bang Bang Boom." "Girl of My Dreams." They were a boy band of brothers—triplets and one older dude. It was the older dude who was with us.

Because of the remote location and the climate, the supply barge can make it to Pangnirtung only once a year. It brings school supplies, canned goods, Christmas decorations—everything the people in town need to survive the year. And every year when the barge arrives, there's a party that lasts three days. I love that image so much. Imagine the feeling of seeing the bow of that barge round the corner and come into sight, carrying everything you'd ever dreamed of. How exciting.

Northern Gotta Do's

BURN down the ice highway from Inuvik out to Tuktoyaktuk and get yourself a Tuk U shirt. It's a fictitious institution with a funny name.

POUND a drink at the Wildcat Cafe in Yellowknife. It's a staple.

SCARF down some fish and chips at Bullocks in Old Town, Yellowknife. Sign the wall while you're there!

STRUT into the Gold Range Saloon in Yellowknife, but be prepared to swap stories—and potentially blows—with one of the testy regulars.

TAKE A RIP out to Behchoko. Takes an hour in the summer and fifteen minutes in the winter on the ice highway. There's a lovely community centre right on the water. You can feel the history of the place.

SCORE some exquisite locally made mukluks, moccasins and mittens at the Gallery of the Midnight Sun in Old Town, Yellowknife. (**Torrens:** I bought Mrs. T. a beautiful blue sheared-beaver scarf there.)

Religious or not, **GO** to a service at the Igloo Church in Inuvik. As part of the tour, make sure you check out the hockey stick shrine in the loft. Make sure to ask how it's heated.

SHRED the caribou medallion at the Granite Room at Discovery Lodge in Iqaluit. It's on the pricey side, but the comfort in your belly will quickly ease the pain in your pocketbook.

HAMMER a golf ball in Holman. Believe it or not, some of the best golfers I've ever seen are there. Kids can hit the ball 250-plus yards in the air off portable pieces of turf. Finding the ball among the rocks on the beach proves to be a bit of a challenge, but twenty-four-hour sunlight helps with that.

In short, just **GO**. Cambridge Bay, Rankin Inlet, Kugluktuk. Every community has its own charm. But make sure you leave an extra day or two at the end. Most of these are fly-in communities, and the weather can wreak havoc with arrival and departure times.

AmeriCanadianity: Us in the US

My Hazy Daze in LA

Taggart

You don't know how great Canada is until you live in another country. I found this out after trying California on for size. I moved down there in 2002 for a couple of years. I was always intrigued by the weather and the flourishing music scene. I had a bunch of friends who had made the leap and seemed to love it. I moved in with a couple NHL players in Manhattan Beach—Sean Avery and Brad Norton.

I met Sean in Detroit when he was playing with the Red Wings. Aves is pretty famed for his brat chatter and legendary party planning, which I thought would keep it entertaining if I lived with him. It certainly was that. I would call those couple of years my lost weekend, a pure blur.

We would have parties most nights, and go find them on other nights. If the Kings were on the road, I would continue the party on my own with my musician bahds, mostly Stacy Jones and Jason Sutter, two great friends whom I'd met years earlier on the road. We got into all kinds of madness together, haunting bars and laughing 'til we cried, mostly. I remember a particular evening in the Valley with Jason. I was going to crash at his place, and he warned me that his roommate had to get up early the next morning for work, so I had to be quiet and respectful when we got back. I told Jason that wouldn't be a problem—I would just crash on the couch without making a peep.

We went to Casa Vega, a great Mexican place known for its margaritas. We got pretty banged up. So banged up that we decided to go to a Mexican strip club. It was full of locals who weren't too pleased with two rock dudes rolling in and laughing it up crosseyed. The mood started to get a little tense when I made it rain with crumpled dollar bills, hollering and laughing like a hyena. We were getting some nasty looks and Jason was smart enough to get me out of there before I got both of us beaten to a pulp. We split and got a cab back to Jason's place.

On the way, he reminded me that I had to keep it down and not wake up his roomie. I set up on the couch and Jason went to his room. All set and time to shut it down, right? Wrong. Jason told me the next morning what happened next, because I don't remember. Apparently, just as J was about to pass out, he heard a scream from his roommate, followed by a yelling match between him and me. I guess I had decided the couch wasn't comfy enough and barged into the other bedroom, hopped in, and when the guy freaked out, I told him to relax, I was just going to sleep. He had no idea who I was, and he lost it. I kept telling him to keep it down or nobody was gonna get any sleep. He couldn't believe what I was doing. I told him there was plenty of room, and to relax.

I can't believe I did that. When Jason told me the next morning, I just about died from embarrassment. The guy had gone to work and was probably dead from lack of sleep. Talk about ridiculous. I never met the guy again after that. I would have liked to apologize, but he was better off with me not bothering and just keeping my distance. Sorry, bahd!

The Keg

Taggart

The second year in, I moved into a beach house with Aves. It was a beautiful place a couple blocks from the previous pad in Manhattan Beach. At this point, I was getting a bit out of hand with drinking. I was blasting Neil Young records from his mid-'70s binge period as the soundtrack. Our neighbours hated us. *The Last Waltz* and *The Richard Pryor Show* were on the TV constantly all through the night. I don't know how many times I woke up to the sound of people from the neighbourhood pounding on the door to tell me to shut it off. It was a messy time for me, fairly dark and damaging.

One weekend we planned a huge shaker, tons of snacks and a keg. Aves was dating Rachel Hunter at the time and it was pretty early in their relationship, so he was running around the world at the drop of a hat with her. Just as we were going to get the party started, he bailed to Paris or something, so the bash was postponed. I decided to see if I could take down that keg by myself, just for kicks. Just so you know, a keg contains almost seven cases of beer— 6.8 to be exact. Or 58.7 litres. Or 165 cans.

This keg was my main source of nutrition for this experiment. It was sitting in the water fountain in the backyard. I would go back, hold the trigger to my lips and jet the ice-cold suds down my throat until I froze inside and couldn't take anymore. It was *so* cold! I would try solo keg stands, just for a morale boost, every few minutes 'til I was shittered, and then have a few more rips until I passed out.

This went on and on. I thought it would only take a few days, but I really started getting into a haze. I'd stumble down to the beach, looking for a good time, but nobody wanted anything to do with me. Everyone assumed I was homeless and troubled. Four or five days into my experiment, I needed to eat something other than a can of beans from the cupboard. So I went up to the main drag of Manhattan Beach to find some real eats. I wandered into a sandwich place and stared at the chalkboard menu. The shop was owned by an older European gentleman who was looking me up and down while I gazed at the options. He asked me what I wanted, but I was so far gone that it was hard for me to speak.

I'm sure the guy thought I was homeless and mentally challenged, rather than drunk. He read me the items on the board and told me to point at what I wanted. I was so hungry, and there was a blackened chicken sandwich that was screaming at me from the board. He sat me down and brought it over to me. As I started eating, I couldn't help noticing the guy crying. He was so happy that I was eating.

I still remember how fuckin' good that chicken sandwich was. I was eating it like Oliver Twist in the workhouse. All I had on were shorts and flops. Greasy. I finished, and he was still teary-eyed as I left with a weak wave. He was such a bahd.

I went back to the house and the keg. I kept on pulling that trigger and hoping I would hear that puff of air, telling me the keg was dead. Approximately five and a half days after I started, I finally heard the *pfffffffftt* of victory. I, Jeremy Taggart, had finally crushed that keg on my own. Talk about small victories.

From that point on in Manhattan Beach, I kept clear of that sandwich shop. I didn't want that bahd to see me straight. He had been so nice to me, I couldn't bear the thought of him thinking I was just banged up. What a sandwich!

As much as I was enjoying the weather and friends in LA, I was starting to feel really empty inside. I missed my home. I missed the changing of seasons. I missed the cheesy TV. I needed Canada back. The drinking was getting old pretty quick, with the sad-sack hangovers and the gurgle guts and "Have you got any Tums?" lifestyle. It was time to go home and get my shit together.

Thankfully, I did.

I moved back home in the late summer of 2004. That winter was a knee-knocker for me. I'd successfully avoided four winters by recording in Hawaii and Vancouver. I was running like T.J. Hooker from cabs to restaurants avoiding the cold. It took me a while to acclimatize, but I grew back my love for winter and I've never looked back. I lost my desire to find another place to live. My comfort for Canada blossomed, I got into a real groove, and within two years I met the love of my life, Lisa, and we started a wonderful family to the tune of two little boys, John and Jack, and our little girl, Aneliese.

Life has changed a lot in the last ten years or so. The clocks whirr at lightning speed, but having a great family with kids who like to party and get banged up on pizza and Chicago mix helps break up the whip of time.

Sink or Schwim

Torrens

How did I end up in the US?

Truth is, after five seasons of *Jonovision* I asked the CBC if we could move the show to a time slot after the news. My feeling was that the audience that had started watching me on *Street Cents* was now, like I was, approaching thirty. Why not keep doing the same show, but a little older, a little later?

There was a feeling internally that I hadn't proven I could carry a show by myself. And that "Canada" wouldn't be able to perceive me as an adult performer because I was so associated with being a kids show guy.

So when I turned thirty I moved to Los Angeles. Partly out of self-imposed exile, because I'd been at the CBC for fifteen years and even I was sick of me. Partly to help turn the page between kids TV host and grown-up. And partly "just to see."

Again with the curiosity.

I had so many preconceived notions about LA, but was wrong on just about every one. Admittedly, I might have formed my opinion based on the montage in *Pretty Woman* where Richard Gere is driving around Beverly Hills.

I thought several things:

- that everyone was loaded and had implants;
- that all dogs had diamond collars;
- that the place was crawling with wide-eyed ingenues and sleazy agents;
- and, maybe most erroneous of all, that there was an open-door policy for Canadian talent, based on the success of Mike Myers and Jim Carrey.

So naive, right? Somehow, deep down, I really expected to be ushered into a studio lot right away. "Thank God you're finally here, Jonathan Torrens. We've been expecting you!"

This was not the case. But none of my other expectations was accurate either.

If you've never been, LA is a big city of small towns, and your experience there depends on which part of the city you live in. Fortunately, a friend of mine had a brother there—a guy I'll call Russ Cochrane, because that was his name—who was more than happy to show me the ropes. He and his partner, Meline, lived in Venice Beach, so that's where I settled. Russ is a screenwriter and great dude who has since gone on to work on *Rookie Blue* and *Orphan Black*. Maybe he just works on shows with colours in the title. Meline took surfing as a course at Santa Monica College. How rad is that?

There's a Main Street in Venice, where people smile and say hello when they pass. There's green space and grocery stores and people with non-showbiz jobs who live and work there. There's a farmers' market where families gather in the sun every Sunday. Sounds so obvious now (and a little hick-ish), but at first everything was so new. I was most surprised by what LA wasn't.

If you'd asked me at the time, I would've told you that I went down there to see if I could make it. Worst-case scenario would be that I'd have this whole new level of credibility back in Canada for having lived in LA. Sad, but true.

The truth is, I was older than most and less ambitious than many when I went. I didn't feel the pull to be a "star," so the idea of a part consisting of five lines on *Moesha* didn't get me out of bed in the morning. After all, I'd already been working on TV series steadily since I was fifteen.

One of the career challenges I've always faced lay in what to call myself. I'm not a standup comic, nor am I a dramatic actor, though I've tried being both. There are so many people who are better at hosting than me, though I've done it. I've done sketch characters, but I'm not an improviser. I'm kind of a . . . comedic performer.

You can be a hybrid in Canada. The market is small enough that you almost have to be able to do a few different things. I've been a dog wrangler, an assistant director, a driver, a writer, a producer, an extra . . .

In LA, they want to know: Are you Seacrest or Schwimmer? You can't be "an actor, who's done a bit of sketch and hosted-ish."

What I didn't anticipate was just how much I'd like it there. The stereotypes do exist—desperate do-anything-to-succeed types—but I was surprised to discover that it's also populated with people who are curious, motivated, ambitious, creative and free-spirited enough to roll the dice on a crazy dream.

University wasn't in the cards for me, and it felt like LA was my higher education. It was more expensive and less guaranteed, but I didn't just find my people there. I found myself.

Honestly, two lessons that I learned there changed my life.

Self-Deprecating Self-Confidence

When you're from Canada—the East Coast specifically—there's a good chance you're self-deprecating. It's who we are. There's nothing worse than a show-off in this part of the world. As my friend Sherry White, who's a Newfoundlander, says, "In junior high, if someone complimented you on your shirt, you'd better say you found it in a dumpster or you'd be accused of showing off."

It's so true.

So when I went to Los Angeles with my pretty solid demo reel from years of characters and hosting bits on *Jonovision*, the executives I met with would say, "We watched your reel. It's good!"

And I'd say. "What? *Really?* No. Well, I guess if you've been working for fifteen years and you can't cobble together a decent three minutes, then you're in the wrong game, amirite?"

You can imagine how confounding this was to Hollywood types. Hollywood is home to the fake-it-'til-you-make-it set. Their faces would contort as they tried to imagine why I'd sabotage my own meeting.

Finally, one of them was kind enough to say, "A compliment is like a gift. When you give your aunt a sweater for Christmas, what do you want her to say?"

"Thank you?" I offered meekly.

"Exactly. You don't want her to say she's pudgy, or allergic, or doesn't look good in robin's-egg blue, you want her to say *thank you.*"

Total light-bulb moment. We see self-confidence as a bad thing, when really all it means is being confident in one's self. The ability to say "thank you" has served me so well. The truth is, if you're not buying your own hype, why would anyone else buy it? Especially important for a salesperson, which is effectively what we "comedic performers" are.

If You're Going to Try to "Make It," Define for Yourself What "It" Is

No matter what business you're in. As I mentioned, I moved to California just to see what would happen. For a laugh. For a lark. To see if I could make it.

It took a few years, some awful auditions and many thousands of dollars (which I consider my student loan) to figure this out. For me, "it" is balance. Between city and country, work and play, staying in and going out, night and day, I couldn't achieve my "it" in Los Angeles. I had to rely on too many other people to define it and let me know how to get it.

I actually don't want it, in showbiz terms. Never really have. I want it on my terms, which is why *Taggart & Torrens* is so satisfying. We created it, and it's exactly what we wanted it to be.

I'm so thankful that I went, though, because I answered the important "what if" question. I'll never wonder what would have happened if I'd gone there. I now know what would happen.

I worked a fair bit on TV shows I'm proud of. Made friends for life. Enjoyed the lifestyle that a warm climate offers. But I also missed Tim Hortons. Putting *u*'s where you don't expect them in words. Personal safety, something we take for granted in Canada.

In the last months I lived in LA, I was escorted a few times from my parking space to my back door by a cop with his weapon drawn because there was "someone on the loose in the neighbourhood" and they were just taking extra precautions.

America's Cutest Puppies

Torrens

My decision to move back really came down to the work, though. I'm terrible at auditioning. Just dreadful. Mostly because I haven't done it much, but also because of my apologetic nature.

My manager thought I should get a commercial agent just to develop better audition skills. Man, if you ever want to feel small, stand in a room with eight other dudes who sort of look like you and say, "*Mmmmm,* Applebee's!" while a group of people behind a table eat salad and judge you.

The older I get, the more value I see in realizing what you're *not* good at. I am not good at commercials. Every time I said something like, "Scotts Turf Builder . . . look at it grow!" or whatever it was, I felt like I needed a tongue-scraper. Just gross inside. Not because the notion of doing commercials doesn't appeal—more because I was so terrible at it. I have a whole new appreciation for people who can take a swig of Sprite Zero, look at the camera and *beam.*

Turns out I don't have a very good poker face for someone who's supposed to be an actor.

There was a commercial audition for some casino in Nevada way out in the Valley one day. The drive from Venice to the Valley takes an hour at best, but with traffic it's often closer to two.

It was a hot day and I was sweating by the time I walked into this dingy, nondescript warehouse building. A man not unlike Larry from *Three's Company* ushered me into a mangy room and "teed up the spot" for me.

Here's the Dilly Bar. (Remember those? How funny was "Home of the Big Brazier" when you were little?)

"All right, *Janathan*, you're at a casino and you're *on fiah*! All your old friends are cheering and all your new friends can't take their eyes off you because who doesn't love a *winnah*? I want you to toss the dice down the table and *bam*, you won again! Really show me that winning smile. Got it? I'll turn some music on to get you in the zone."

Larry cranked some bad synth music and gave me the high sign that we were rolling. Now, as bad as I used to be at fake laughing, I'm so much worse at fake smiling. I don't smile easily and find it really difficult to be genuine in a contrived circumstance.

Plus, here's the thing. My friends *weren't* there. I *wasn't* winning. I was alone with Larry in a carpeted room deep in the Valley and looking at rush-hour traffic to get back to Venice, all for this.

So I blew into my empty hand for good luck and fired the imaginary dice down the table. I paused for a second, then made a noise that could only be described as "*Wheeeeeooooooahhhh!*" Kind of like Al Pacino in *Scent of a Woman*.

Larry paused the music. He was disappointed in me.

"I'm not buying it yet, *Janathan*. I really need to see that you're killing it. Let's do it again, and I'll even crank the music to get you pumped."

I blew again. I threw again. And I yelled "*I'm dying inside!*" over the music.

Grooving along, Larry turned the music down and asked what I'd said.

"*Nothing*," I responded, walking out of the room before the tape had even stopped rolling.

Now, if *I* were casting that commercial, I'd have given it to me.

You get into this weird mindset where you're waiting for the phone to ring for jobs you wouldn't want to do anyway—"Why haven't the casino people called?!"

There were some memorably bad auditions. The one with Tori Spelling, where I was asked to not make direct eye contact with her . . . even though it was an intimate scene. No problem. She looks a bit like a sculpin. I snuck a peek.

The one for a reality show called *Housebusters*. Let's say you've suffered a recent tragedy in your home. A team of psychics, interior decorators and feng shui experts will smudge the demons and give your place a bit of a facelift.

I swear to God, this was part of the audition: "Becky, I know this is hard for you because your roommate just committed suicide here in your living room . . . but have you ever thought of purple accent cushions?"

Walked out of that one too.

Then there was the audition for the Jeff Foxworthy Blue Collar Comedy thingamabobby. They asked everyone to come in with a "Southern character." Strategizing at home the night before, I assumed that everyone would come in with the same RickyBobbyHickyKnobby thing, so I planned to make my character pop.

My character would be Jebediah Jameson, the only albino black man from the great state of Louisiana.

It seemed so funny and original to me, given my colouring and non-racist intentions. Jebediah's voice was deep and whisky-soaked; his tale was heartwarming. *Good for me*, I thought, *I'm thinking outside the box.*

The next day, my first character or two went pretty well, and I'd saved Jebediah for my big finish. I'll never forget their faces, slowly sinking, their eyes shifting uncomfortably to the ground. Staring at the floor, avoiding eye contact even as I apologized *during* the audition and assured them it was almost over.

But even that one wasn't the worst, I'm afraid. No. The worst was *America's Cutest Puppies*.

Imagine standing in a tux in front of eight cameras and America, sharing the information that "tonight, the K-9 fur-nalists move into the Dog House. America, the phone lines are open. Who will advance? Patches? Mittens? Tim?"

Not actually sure which is worse—not getting the gig, or getting it and having to show up every week and try to sell it. And then put *America's Cutest Puppies* on your resumé.

I left the audition and called my mom to keep me company on the long drive back to Venice. She had a dentist's appointment the next day and was scared to go. She doesn't like dentists and had no one to take her.

That's when it hit me like a ton of bricks. At the end of my life, would I rather be the guy who took his mom to the dentist because she was scared or that guy from *America's Cutest Puppies*?

Easy choice. And not just because the *Puppies* people never called.

It just wasn't me. The faking it. The backslapping and going to a bar because so-and-so might be there. The "Seacrest or Schwimmer" dilemma.

Every casting room I was in, the casting director would look at the other dudes in tight V-neck T-shirts and say, "You guys will read for the hunk," and then at me and say, "You'll read for the perv, the effeminate guy at the office and the weird neighbour."

I was never going to be the mysterious drifter in an ABC pilot. As Jer would say, whatev-salad.

Waaaaahn Waaaaahn

Torrens

 You know what? In Canada, I can be both Seacrest *and* Schwimmer. I can be J-Roc and *Jonovision*, *Street Cents* and *Taggart & Torrens*. Here I have access to people at networks who can run with an idea or give honest feedback as to why it's not a good fit.

My manager used to say, "No is the second-best answer in Hollywood," and he's right. Knowing is so much better than not knowing, and in LA you rely on so many people who'll let you know when they know.

Also, in Canada I can live out in the country, go to Sobeys for groceries and take my kids to school. During my time in the US I was exposed to several A-listers whose lives just seemed dreadful. They are trapped, lonely humans.

When you're a character performer, you need real-life experience to draw on. Living where I do, I have that. I'm famous in my neighbourhood—mostly for being the guy who doesn't know how to do a single thing for himself.

Best of all, in LA I got a professional page turn. I came back to Canada a grown-up and was ready to take my next step.

See, when I was in the States, I always knew at some point I'd be back in Canada, and I toyed with the idea of what would be a good fit.

The CBC was working on a remake of *Front Page Challenge*, the news quiz show that was so popular back in the '60s. They contacted my manager to ask if I'd be interested in auditioning to host.

My feeling was that it wasn't the right fit, but my manager argued otherwise. His feeling was that unless you are morally opposed to what's being asked of you, you might as well do it because you never know when this producer and that director might work together on something else, blah blah blah.

Fine. I bought into that logic. Even though I was pretty sure hosting *Front Page Challenge* wasn't the move for me, I agreed to audition. To be clear, I didn't think for a moment I was above it. As a freelancer, you're not wired to say no to a job. You assume every one will be your last. I just wasn't sure if the show was right for me. There were so many other candidates I would've suggested for such an important role.

Then, a couple of days later, the CBC called my manager again and said they were conducting what they called "chemistry tests"—pairing up this host with that panel, this group of panellists together, that kind of thing. They were wondering if I would also audition as a panellist.

After thinking about it, it just didn't sit well. It was never my way to lead anyone on, and I just thought it was best to be upfront from the get-go. That way, it wouldn't put me in a relationship-damaging position if they did offer me a panellist position and I said no. After all, I'd spent more of my life at the CBC than anywhere else and really valued the relationship. Still do.

So I told my manager in an email that I'd be happy to tell the CBC that it wasn't a good fit, or he could, but I just didn't want to string them along in any way. It just seemed like the professional approach. Twenty seconds after I hit send, I got an email back from him that said, quote, "Waaaaahn waaaaahn my pussy hurts! i don't want to be a f*cking panellist!"

Followed by another email that read, "Sorry Jono, that email was intended for my assistant."

Nice cover! Don't you hate that? When people put you in a position that makes you have to either (a) look stunned or (b) call them on their stuff?

I debated what to do. And then I opted to do *nothing* for twenty-four hours while his emails and phone messages piled up, after which I wrote him a brief email in which I again explained my decision to be straight up with the CBC. I was particularly proud of my sign off.

"Well, better run . . . off to my appointment with the gynecologist!"

Another good lesson learned: I don't put the person's address in any email message until I'm good and ready to send it. If it's a testy one especially, I write it in the exact language I'm feeling in that moment and then wait twenty-four hours. If I still feel that way, I'll send it. But I usually don't. As my mother-in-law says, you can't take back anything you put down in writing. She also says, "The second you raise your voice, you've lost the argument."

Smart woman. It's true: there's no more powerful negotiating tactic than genuine indifference. Not caring actually makes it kind of fun and often works out in your favour anyway. If people think they can't have you, they suddenly have to.

I don't have an agent or manager now, and it works in my favour. First, because it makes people uncomfortable to deal with me directly on money issues. And second, because why give away pieces of your small-enough-as-it-is pie if you don't have to?

Bonus tip: use this the next time you negotiate a much-deserved raise with your boss. *Silence.* It's an old interviewing technique that works especially well over the phone. The laws of social grace that apply to a conversation don't apply to negotiating, and it's the same with an interview. So if your boss says, "I'd like to offer you fifty dollars extra per week," just say nothing. *Tick-tock-tick*. It's scary and thrilling, but if you keep quiet I guarantee they'll jump in with something like "Of course, this is just a starting point."

John Dunsworth, who plays Mr. Lahey on *Trailer Park Boys*, has a variation on this theme. He just repeats exactly what the person has said, with no emotion at all.

"We'd like to offer you a thousand dollars."

"A thousand dollars," John repeats, totally deadpan.

"Yes," they say.

Beat.

"Or maybe two thousand is more in the ballpark, is it?"

Trust me. It works.

FAQ: OLP and TPB

When You Know It's Time to Go

Taggart

Life is about learning and giving/getting love, and trying to find a balance of happiness in the face of hard work. When I started drumming, I did it because it gave me an instant connection to an incredible feeling: playing time. When you play time, you are gone. A total escape to an unexplained paradise. It's a pure feeling, like you're speaking a foreign language, learning new phrases and conversing to no end. The more you work on the craft, the better the conversation becomes. By the time you become well versed on your instrument, it's a well-oiled, polished language that is entirely you. Impossible to be anyone else. Therefore perfect, in my humble opinion. The further you take your own language, the bigger you make yourself sound, projecting this giant vocabulary built for time. You are deluxe.

When you join a band, that same formula is what it takes for a band to be great. You need to weave each instrument into the others and create a fabric that is fresh and interesting. Then you take that to market, to sell your brand in the mass-media motorway.

When OLP started, we did exactly that. We hunkered down in a warehouse somewhere in Mississauga, writing songs for twelve hours a day, seven days a week. We pounded the pavement for weeks, crafting music that we thought was different and exciting. When we were getting close to having enough songs for an album, we finally felt like a real band, and once we started recording those songs, we knew we had something special, something to be proud of. A reason to exist! I had just turned eighteen, so I was over the moon.

I was living with my folks in Weston at the time, and things weren't very good. We were living in a one-bedroom apartment— my two brothers, Jetsun and James, and me in the bedroom, while my folks, Ronnie and Beryl, rocked a foam mattress on the floor of the living room each night. My sister, Jenni, had already flown the coop and lived down the street with her new husband. Times were tight and tightening.

I was so amped when got our initial advance from Sony. It was a small deal back then, seven albums (which we completed—a rare feat!), with reasonable budgets for each album, escalating if we sold records. We started to pay ourselves $150 per week. I had only been a dishwasher at Reggie's Sandwich Factory in Barrie, a job that I worked at for just two weeks before quitting, citing fun in the summer as my reason. So this was real money for me. I felt like I was rolling in dough.

Everything was happening at once. I'll never forget those days—I was so young and put forth my best maturity to fit in with all these new adults in my life. My grandmother, who was the matriarch of the Taggart family, was so happy for me. I remember telling her I had this new band with a real record label, and we were going to get a real shot, and I was really into the music we were making. I still remember how proud she was, telling everyone about how great it was going to be for me. She passed away before we got into the studio, but I always felt her love and confidence with every step. She knew we were gonna blow up. Her blessing was enormous.

Naveed came out in spring of 1994 and got, I would say, a good response in Canada. We had great success in Quebec, because MusiquePlus put our first single, "The Birdman," into extreme heavy rotation—maybe because we did our initial touring in small towns around Quebec, who knows. I'm just glad we had a buzz somewhere.

But *Naveed* didn't blow up until it came out in the States the following spring. When KROQ in LA decided to spin "Starseed" a lot, that's when the wheels started ripping. We caught fire in Boston on WBCN, much thanks to radio legend and early OLP bahd Carter Alan. WBRU in Providence also burned it, and we had great support in Atlanta at 99X. To get the blessing from all these influential stations meant everything. All of a sudden, we were being accepted in Canada as the next big thing in America, and we all know how horny that makes Canadian programmers. Our airplay grew tenfold across the board in Canada on radio and MuchMusic.

From that point on, I think we had a video in heavy rotation consistently for the next seven years! It's interesting how it takes America's attention to validate something in Canada. I hope that eases at some point, so we can have the sack to accept something as our own without the need for it first to find acceptance with Uncle Sam.

That initial buzz from the States was so intoxicating; we chased it like a donkey after a dangled carrot for the rest of my days in OLP. It was quite crippling in many ways. To start something on the basis of pure expression and individuality, but then respect boundaries that are created and imposed by modern radio is, to me, a serpent eating its own tail. And that can be very frustrating indeed. To change in spite of your gut instinct, or ignore it completely, is very difficult and dangerous. You become too much like your surroundings and you shallow out. It's not easy, and probably necessary to prolong a career, but it's completely alien to me. I'm not good at it. I know this 100 percent because I tried and tried.

When I decided to leave OLP, I was really starting to feel blind in too many ways. I didn't understand how things were happening, and I was tired of arguing about which way the ship should sail. Twenty-one years is a long time to do anything—a very long time. I felt it was time to get control of my own life, and the moment I decided this was to be, I felt the release of something huge come away and off me. I know from that feeling that I made the right decision. Never ignore your instincts, bahds. They're all we really have to find our way in the world.

Trailer Park Boys II Men

Torrens

In the spring of 2016, *Trailer Park Boys* was renewed by Netflix for its eleventh season. There was so much to like about the Netflix experience. No executive in charge giving inane notes. They really trust the key creatives to make the show they bought in the first place. It's awesome, actually, the way they've raised the bar for other networks, because the traditional development system doesn't work so well in Canada.

To tell the truth, I'd made my mind up to leave the show when Clattenburg left right after the third movie. He'd brought me in originally, and I felt pretty happy with what I'd accomplished with the character. Again, it's the delicate dance between maximizing an opportunity and leaving the door open for others. I didn't want to be J-Roc for the rest of my life. There were other voices, other characters in my head that wanted out.

But I admired the three boys for taking a giant leap and acquiring the rights to the series. They'd been out on the road and were convinced that there was still an appetite for the show.

They were right. In fact, you could argue that once it landed on Netflix, it really started to take off. Around the world, certainly.

The three guys complement each other very well in that *Wizard of Oz* kind of way. Mike has courage. Robb has brains. John Paul has heart. Together, they cover all the bases, but some fans would argue it was best when there was a wizard named Mike Clattenburg working his magic behind the scenes.

It's fairly evident in the later seasons that Mike Smith has a darker, more shock-oriented sense of humour than Clattenburg. Clattenburg softened the hard edges with kitties, gut slaps and genuine love. Smith can be raunchier and more prone to sexual gags and visual-anatomy humour—people pooing themselves, boners and such.

No question he's a great writer, though, with a very strong sense of story and flow.

I was on the fence about coming back when they asked, even though playing that character is one of the most fun things I've ever done and the three guys are all genuinely fun to be around. Somehow, the show itself was always bigger than the sum of its sometimes-dysfunctional parts.

I initially said no, but Mike Smith asked if I would shoot a few days just to explain what happened to the character. That seemed like a reasonable request, so I agreed. That was season 8.

When the show was picked up yet again for season 9, I intended to say no. Carole and I were talking about it and—like a good partner does—she said, "I feel like it's my job to point out that you came home beaming from each of those days you did last year. Say no if you want, but maybe ask yourself why it is you're saying no."

She was right. As she so often is. It *was* fun.

I realized that my reluctance was rooted in worry that Mike Clattenburg and Mike Volpe (my good friend and producer of *Mr. D*) would feel slighted or betrayed. So I told both of them about my concerns and that I was choosing to do *Trailer Park Boys*, but I wasn't picking sides and I hoped it was okay, but it was shooting near my house and I had a family to feed, and, and, and . . .

They were both perfect gentlemen about it and immediately endorsed my decision. Clattenburg went so far as to say he was glad I'd be involved. True class.

So I jumped into season 9 with vigour. I was back in the writer's room and even directed a few episodes. Talk about big shoes to fill, but I'd learned a lot by osmosis from watching Clatty all those years. Plus, if ever there was an aesthetic I could achieve, it had to be that one.

We gave J-Roc a kid named M.C. Flurry, which felt like great new territory to pursue. J-Roc as a new dad mirrored my real-life experience, and it felt like there was a lot to play there. It played out like an ABC after-school special in J-Roc's unique patois.

In season 10 we elevated J-Roc's storyline again, giving him a new wife from Mexico called Marsha, and now he had to balance the relationships in his new blended family. We added the risky but challenging layer of Marsha not knowing he wasn't Hispanic, so he had to speak with a Spanish accent in front of her. Definitely high concept, but most fans of the show seemed to really dig it.

If I'm being honest, a nagging feeling started to gnaw at me during season 10. It felt like the agenda of the show was starting to collide with the personal agendas of those who made it, resulting in some curious creative choices. Getting Snoop Dogg to be on the show was a coup, I guess, but seemed to me, at least, like quite a shoehorn from a plausibility standpoint. Same with Jimmy Kimmel appearing via Skype. Pretty hard to justify that under the umbrella of likely. Then Tom Arnold was added to the cast. Then weed comic Doug Benson.

My first instinct was that maybe Snoop could play Calvin, some-one's cousin from away. To me, that would've been so much cooler. Have Snoop on playing against type, but never shine a light on his real identity.

Don't get me wrong—it's cool and inconceivable that these folks even know about the show, let alone dig it. But it felt a bit like grandstanding for the sole purpose of saying, "Look who we know!" When season 10 came out, reaction among diehard *TPB* fans to the celebrity cameo factor seemed mixed.

But one thing the three guys know about is their brand and how to maximize it. There's no denying these high-profile names extended the show's reach. Snoop was a super-nice guy and his posse was awesome. It was actually really fun to have them around. Tom Arnold was maybe the biggest surprise for me. He's kind, humble and *funny*. We'd never had that gear on the show before, the "holy shit this place is awful," wide-eyed wonder.

I wasn't asked back in the writer's room for season 11. Maybe because I flagged my discomfort at a few of the things I thought crossed the line, maybe because I was verbal about feeling lukewarm towards the cameos. Maybe because I'm not a good writer. In any event, I had a brief email exchange with Smith about what the boys saw J-Roc doing in season 11 and it sounded like there would be no Marsha, no Flurry, just back to rolling with T. There was some mention of there being a strip club where they would work. I wasn't sure how J-Roc could just go back to pre-family styles.

As I was trying to somehow get psyched for season 11, there were some unfortunate high-profile off-screen occurrences involving cast members. It's not my place to go into them in detail here, but it's relevant for context because they definitely factored into my decision to leave the show.

One of my side hustles is corporate hosting work in the States, and when these conservative companies started hearing about these antics, they questioned whether they should remain associated with me, someone from the show. They were suddenly asking me not to mention my affiliation with *TPB*. It became very uncomfortable. These gigs provide a great revenue stream for me and my family that may last for another twenty years. Nothing is worth jeopardizing that. What it comes down to is if I'm up for a gig against someone else who doesn't have that potentially negative association, all things otherwise being equal, I'd lose out every time. There's enough risk in corporate America. Booking some guy as a host who is part of a show that's been in the headlines for suspect reasons simply isn't worth it.

Look, lots of people have asked if there was one specific thing that led to my departure. The short answer is no. There were several small things that added up to one crystal-clear decision.

And so, after ten seasons, three movies, two specials and more laughs than I could ever count, I made the decision to hang up the ol' do-rag.

Clear and direct communication has always been a problem that plagued *Trailer Park Boys*. Like in many workplaces, whispered fractured conversations take the place of outward ones. This breeds paranoia and leaves people feeling out of the loop or even unaware of what the common goal is. That's dangerous in any environment, but especially in a creative one.

In this case, I had a great conversation with the three guys. Really great. Candid and respectful, as gentlemen and friends. I prefaced it by saying a hard conversation is so much better than not having one, and they seemed to agree. I started by saying that what anyone does in their private life is none of my concern, other than I'm genuinely worried about people I care about. But it becomes my business when it affects my income and reputation. We volleyed the tricky situation back and forth to work out a way forward and arrived at a satisfactory conclusion that would see me still involved, but to a lesser degree. I was happy with that, and they said they were too.

Later that day, I heard from their producer that there had been a change of heart about the course of action we'd all agreed on hours before.

I copied the guys on my response, reinforcing that we'd all agreed just that morning on the importance of clear and direct communication, but I never heard back from them.

Actually, I got an email from J.P. on the side a couple of days later. The heart. Hoping things were cool.

Things are cool. I don't regret my decision to leave even one bit, and it's certainly not like the entire franchise hinged on my being there. It's my prerogative to see what else is out there, just as much as it's theirs to suck the marrow out of that *TPB* bone until it cracks.

The biggest lesson I've learned in life and in my professional career is to calmly and respectfully speak one's mind. It's show *business*, not show feelings.

It's weird how sometimes we get into the habit of not saying anything because we don't want to hurt someone's feelings, but it ends up being way worse in the long run. That tack never works.

In life, in work, in relationships, you might as well say what you're thinking, because that's the stuff that will eat you alive.

Fans of the show were very kind (for the most part) in wishing me well and thanking me for the memories the character had made for them. It was overwhelming, actually, the impact that show had/has on its audience. As I said at the time, the true legacy of *Trailer Park Boys* will always be the loyalty of its fans.

In December 2016, a guy sent me a tweet asking how much he'd have to donate to a shelter to get a signed J-Roc picture. The truth is, I didn't have any pictures, so I replied by saying, "How about this—for anyone who sends proof of a $50 donation to any shelter or food bank, I'll record a custom J-Roc greeting for whoever you want!"

Holy cow, did that thing snowball. That's one of the great things about the internet. The donations started rolling in and people were getting them as Christmas presents. "Can you do one for my cousin Kyle? Make sure to say *mafk!*" "Could you do one for the boys in the fire hall? End it with *Raaaaaaaaaaay!*"

Over the next two weeks, I recorded more than five hundred messages. Mostly as J-Roc, but the odd Gordon Lightfoot or Robert Cheeley (my character on *Mr. D*) too. I sent them to people in eight countries.

And we raised more than $30,000 for food banks and shelters. All because of one tweet. Felt like the perfect way to say goodbye to the character. Nomesayin?

Frig Off, Peckers

Torrens

In the fall of 2016, Taggart and I decided to do a few more *TnT* live dates around the Maritimes. My mother wasn't well so I had to stay relatively local, and by touring the Maritimes I could be within three hours of Halifax if I had to get back for any reason.

With the help of our homie Nick Zildjian, we geared up the Frig Off Peckers tour, named after Andrea's catchphrase, and booked shows in Charlottetown, Fredericton and Halifax.

We really wanted to go to Newfoundland too, but the reality is, it's very cost-prohibitive. We make a bit of cash on some of the dates thanks to merch sales, but it costs a fair bit to fly where we need to be, and then pay the venue and cover expenses like hotels, food and rental cars.

But some things you do for love and some things you do for money. And as someone who grew up in a region that not every band made it to, I know how much that sucks. Plus, if ever there's a place riddled with bahds, it's Newfoundland. So when I found a couple of decently priced flights from Halifax to St. John's, we thought, what the heck. We can't claim we toured the country and preach Canadianity without going from coast to coast, so let's do it.

We booked a show at the Ship Pub and our friends Fortunate Ones helped promote it.

I'd personally been road-banging pretty hard, doing corporates, and had just returned from overseas when Frig Off Peckers started. The ghirlst were still on European time, so they were getting up at four in the morning and the long days were catching up with me.

The first night in Charlottetown was great. It's always fun to be home, and the Prince Edward Island Brewing Company is a wonderful, cozy venue. It was fun to see Taggart face to face, and the adrenalin got us through.

The next day, we drove from PEI to Fredericton and I was starting to lose my voice. I assumed it was just fatigue from a late night and early morning. By five o'clock, though, I couldn't even talk above a whisper. I was lying in my hotel room, trying to decide what to do. Should we cancel? Could we come up with a creative way to do the show that didn't involve me talking? That seemed difficult. But then I saw a tweet from a listener. "Just found a sitter for tonight. Can't wait to see the *bahds!*"

I thought that, given the spirit and warmth of the people who listen and come to our shows, they would understand that this was beyond my control. I'd just be upfront and honest about the situation.

So the show went on. You know what? It was extra special. I started by saying if anyone wanted their money back due to my voice—or lack thereof—they were more than welcome to it. I then plopped a $20 bill on the table in front of us and said the only caveat was that they'd have to come take it during the show.

Ice broken. We played Blank-Lookin' Mafk with whiteboards that Jer and Lisa had scored at Dollarama. We did a sketch where I was the Vannellis' father, so it made sense that I would speak in a whisper. It couldn't have gone better.

The next two shows were in Halifax, at the Seahorse. Another warm, squishy *TnT* venue, like the Carleton, where we had played the last time we were in Halifax.

Some Canadianity for you: the Carleton is run by Mike Campbell of *Mike & Mike's Excellent X-Canada Adventures* fame. That show was one of the early staples on MuchMusic and, in a way, its dynamic was not unlike the one that Jer and I have.

The Seahorse is owned by Victor Syperek, a Hali-famous person who used to work as an art director in film before designing several of Halifax's most famous and gorgeous haunts, the Shoe Shop and the Press Gang among them.

I was happy to be in Halifax for two shows because it's home, but also because it meant I could visit my mom on both days. At the time, Susan was seventy-six. She'd been suffering from Alzheimer's for a couple of years, and though she was a little repetitive and didn't have great problem-solving skills, she still knew who we were and didn't have the angry or disoriented spells that so many Alzheimer's patients and loved ones have to deal with.

We'd also just learned that Susan had a pretty good-sized tumour in her lungs. The doctor felt, as we did, that she didn't have the will or stamina to get treatment, and we were well aware that neither of these issues would get better, only worse.

She had been living in a healthcare facility in Halifax called Northwood Manor for several months. It's a wonderful place where residents live (as opposed to "wait to die"), and the staff there is simply unrivalled. They love the residents. You often see them dancing with them, teasing them, painting their nails. I grew to really love going to visit my mom there because it was so uplifting. But I was feeling some guilt. Here she was, her quality of life diminishing, while I travelled and worked and parented and did whatever else.

There's a hospice coordinator at Northwood whose name is Mary. She might be the person who's most in the job that's right for them that I've ever met in my life.

My sister Marj and I were meeting with her about what to expect and what came next and probable timelines. That kind of stuff. I confessed I was feeling guilty about travelling for work and asked whether I should cancel everything. Mary said that they encourage people in our position to do three things.

1. Tell your loved one exactly how you feel about them every time you see them.
2. Carry on with your life and travels.
3. Tell them where you're going and for how long. That way, if they choose to wait for you to return, they can. But they also may be waiting for you to go away because they don't want you to be around for their departure.

What a mind-blowing moment that was. Thinking about someone "deciding" to go when they were ready gave me such an incredible perspective on life.

I thought about it. I'd always been very vocal about how much I loved my mom. I teased her mercilessly and she loved it. She'd been vocal about how much she adored Carole and the girls. How she was so happy for me that I was so happy.

She didn't want a funeral of any kind. She wanted to donate her body to medical science. There was really nothing I could do except be there for my sister, so that she wasn't forced to hold a vigil alone.

Marj and I went to visit the Susebot on Monday after the Halifax shows. She'd been better, but she'd also been worse. Her words weren't coming all that easily, nor was her breath, but we still had a couple of laughs.

More important, I told her I loved her and that she was a good momma. I kissed her on the forehead when we left.

The next day, Taggart and I flew to St. John's and were picked up by our friends Andrew and Paddy, complete with salt-and-vinnies, beer and a sign that said BAHDS. We checked into our Airbnb, and in typical rock 'n' roll fashion, Jer went to have a nap.

I was debating what to do when I saw that I'd missed a call from Carole. And another from Northwood.

My mom had just died. Peacefully, quickly, relatively painlessly.

The first thing I thought was of what Mary had said: "Maybe she's waiting for you to go away so you don't have to be around for it." I had been away for one night. What are the odds?

I debated what to do. Should I cancel the show? Should I change my flight? Should I tell Taggart?

The answer to all of those questions was no. Rushing home wouldn't change anything. Telling Taggart would only give the night a morbid tone. Cancelling the show wouldn't change the outcome.

Carole offered to come, which was typically perfect of her. Truthfully, I was worried that if I saw her I might break down, and I wanted to get through the show first. And maybe I wasn't sure I could handle that. Plus, I thought, what better place to spend a rainy Tuesday night with like-minded people than the Ship Pub, a classic St. John's destination?

In my head, I decided that the show would be my little tribute to Susan. A wake, if you will. It gave me—and I think the show—a slightly more serious tone, but I've since heard from lots of folks who were there that they had a great time.

If I could go back and change the decisions I made at that time, I wouldn't.

As dreadful as it sounds, the combo of Alzheimer's and lung cancer was actually great in my mom's case. Her brain didn't know what her body was doing. Her body sped up the natural process, so she didn't have to live for fifteen years not knowing who or what we were.

Best of all, I have some fond memories of the slightly kooky super-patient woman who was my mom. I called her many things over the years—Baby Susan, Clammy, Clamsterdam, Clam and Cheese, Susapotamus, Stusant . . . but none of them bugged her more than Dennis.

In my twenties I took to calling my mother that, mostly because it was the unlikeliest nickname. It took off within the family, and soon everyone was calling her Dennis. To the point where it actually stopped being funny and just became reality.

"What time are we going to Dennis's for Thanksgiving?"

"What are you getting Dennis for Christmas?"

There was only one problem—"Dennis" hated it. Like, couldn't stand it. Like, made the sound *accchk* whenever she was called it. She doesn't even like it when people call her Sue. Dennis was like sandpaper on her ears.

During an intense cribbage game at a rented cottage on PEI, she told me she wanted to make a bet. "If I win, you'll never call me 'Dennis' again."

I thought about it. Those were high stakes.

"Fine. But if I win, I never call you 'Mom' for the rest of your life."

She took the bet. And then she skunked me. Dennis was done.

So I waited two weeks and started calling her Reggie.

Canadianity for Dummies

Okay, say you have a dinner party tonight with the family of your hot new Canadian girlfriend, and you want to fit in and keep up. Just read and absorb this next section and you'll be good to go. It's like the Coles Notes of Canadianity. Do you even know what Coles Notes are? Oh man, you're in trouble.

Taggart

Here are some of my favourite Canadian TV shows, the ones that impacted me—and most people—growing up in Canada in the '80s and early '90s.

The Beachcombers

A staple on Sundays in my household. The silly dealings of Nick Adonidas and Relic. The drama of the logging industry in BC. How Canadian is that? Bahds trying to sell logs and foiling the attempts of West Coast crooks. This show was the epitome of

Canadian television. A glimpse of a western small-town location, with the strong brush of whodunit. A classic stew of wholesome Canadianity.

Degrassi Junior High

This show had the most realistic casting. I remember watching *The Kids of Degrassi Street* when I was really young. Kids smoking darts in their greasy little clubhouse hangout. I always remember it feeling so local, like they'd cast kids from my school. Nobody was too pretty or too ugly. The plotlines always featured the worst possible outcomes too, which made it hard to not watch. There was always a train wreck in each episode, somebody going through some sort of hell, like pregnancy or a death in the family.

The Littlest Hobo

Another staple in my house. The sleuthing German shepherd that helped out a person in need, only to dump them at the end of every episode, moving along to the next town to help someone else. When I toured in the US as a kid, I used to bullshit in interviews, saying that I was in that show when I was younger. Haha! I used to say I was in the bulk of the series. Classic. It helped with my homesickness.

Wok with Yan

Another show I used to love watching. The puns on Stephen Yan's aprons were the best. Looking back, I'm pretty sure he made the same dish every episode. He would fire up the wok, cut up some chicken and veggies, douse it with "sesame street" oil, then grab a bahd from the audience to crush it with him at the end. Such a great show.

The Friendly Giant

With his gentle demeanour, Friendly was a total beauty. Hanging out with a rock-hard-looking giraffe and a baggy rooster, telling tales and having laughs. My dad's drum teacher, Howie Ray, was on the show's music staff. I remember him getting pointed out in the credits. It was a big deal. That, and the time my mom had to give up her squirrel monkey as a young girl, so she gave it to *The Uncle Bobby Show*. It was on there for years.

Seeing Things

A cheesy, but serious detective show where Louis Del Grande has the ability to see glimpses of the future, helping him solve crimes. I always thought it was classic when he had visions. It was like he was getting a migraine or something—the pain of seeing into the future! Jonathan has a script from a *Seeing Things* episode from his days at the CBC. That's gold. When Torrens's J-Roc character threw out "Louis Del Grande–lookin' mafk" to Jim Lahey in a *Trailer Park Boys* episode, I died laughing. That's a quality pull right there.

Torrens

It's hard to pick just a handful of shows that have defined this country (and me), but here is a litmus sampling of staples.

Hockey Night in Canada

The opening strains of the theme song—the old one—can give even the least sentimental Canuck full-bodied chills. Ron & Don.

Bob Cole. Jim Hughson. Especially in spring, when the playoffs start, the whole country gets Saturday night fever.

The Tommy Hunter Show/Rita & Friends

I'm throwing these in together because Tommy Hunter and Rita MacNeil did the same thing. Both had CBC variety shows that showcased the best in Canadian music.

Wayne & Shuster

As a kid, the humour was a little lost on me, but even then the chemistry between Johnny Wayne and Frank Shuster was undeniable. Their theme song was also unforgettable!

Speakers' Corner

Maybe Canada's first reality show. For twenty-five cents, citizens could speak their mind in a video booth outside MuchMusic headquarters at the corner of Queen and John in downtown Toronto. The clips were then edited into a half-hour weekly TV show. Not only did it cost Citytv very little to produce, but people *paid* to be on it. Just another example of what a televisionary Moses Znaimer was.

The Kids in the Hall

I watched as a teenage kid with my jaw dropped, intoxicated and invigorated by this absurd troupe of cross-dressing, catch-phrasing, mould-breaking whack jobs. Maybe the most formative inspiring experience of my entire life. Still ahead of the curve, twenty-five years later.

Plot or Not?

Is this a real plot to an episode of one of your favourite classic Canadian TV shows or not?

1. *Beachcombers:* At the grand reopening of Molly's Reach, Nick and Jesse have to make excuses for Relic, who's passed out in the kitchen from drinking too much cooking sherry.

2. *Seeing Things:* Louis Ciccone bears an amazing resemblance to Stefan of Drabvania, but just as he is about to assume the king's identity, the real king is kidnapped and his bodyguard murdered.

3. *Murdoch Mysteries:* Percival Jenkins is found murdered at his breakfast. While questioning the servants, Murdoch discovers that many maids have been let go over the years for their "loose morals."

4. *Degrassi:* Drake's character, Jimmy, takes a Viagra and gets a boner that won't go away for the entire school day.

5. *Street Legal:* Olivia represents a controversial sexist author, but ends up sleeping with him in the judge's chambers.

6. *Heartland:* Ty and Amy arrive home from Calgary to discover that someone has let the horses out of their stalls and an equestrian orgy is in full swing.

7. *My Secret Identity:* Andrew (Jerry O'Connell) must choose between going on a double date and spending time with a troubled boy.

8. *Beachcombers:* Relic mistakes a beekeeper's cargo of honey for gold and fights Nick for possession of it.

The Prize Is Right: Canadian Game Shows

Definition

Cool-as-a-cucumber host Jim Perry gave clues in this hangman-inspired game, where contestants competed to win tens of dollars' worth of prizes. Bic pens! A week's supply of Rice-A-Roni! Bus tickets!

Bumper Stumpers

Al Dubois showed contestants two vanity plates, and they had to guess which one pertained more to an owner he would describe. Wanna play right now?

"Which plate, the left or the right, would be more apt to belong to a speed demon?"

To this day, we can't flip past a rerun. We have to stop and watch. It's like *A Baby Story* on TLC. You know how it's going to end, but you still have to see it through.

I always thought getting LDUBOIS as a personalized plate would be worth it, just to completely blow the minds of both people who got it.

Test Pattern

Turbo-bahd Dan Gallagher co-hosted a lo-fi game show on MuchMusic with Luc Casimiri. Luc is a super-dry Italo-Canadian who has written every award show in Canadian history.

Luc was to *Test Pattern* what Paul Bellini was to *Kids in the Hall*. In a word, essential.

Talk About

Hosted by charming game show staple Wayne Cox, *Talk About* got contestants to do just that: talk about a subject for twenty seconds to see how many relevant words they could utter from a hidden list. "For twenty seconds, talk about . . . *ashtrays!*"

Kidnadianity

Would you believe there were shows for kids other than *Street Cents* and *Jonovision*? If you grew up in Canada, odds are you watched one, some or all of these.

The Friendly Giant

Bob Homme wore felt and invited young viewers to curl up in a tiny chair in his castle and listen to stories. His co-stars were hand puppets Rusty the Rooster and Jerome the Giraffe (allegedly played by the same puppeteer, straddling a post).

Student Bodies

A partly animated *Saved by the Bell* riff about the lives and loves of a group of kids working at the school newspaper.

Catwalk

Neve Campbell and some guy with a curling-rock haircut danced and brooded about teenage issues.

The Raccoons

A cartoon series about a group of pests led by Cyril Sneer.

Danger Bay

Christopher Crabbe, Ocean Hellman and other people with less sea-faring names, like Donnelly Rhodes, rescued marine animals in BC.

The Edison Twins

They were really smart and solved mysteries. Worth a watch now for the '80s clothes and the chance to spot cameos by then up-and-coming Canadian actors.

Today's Special

Ontarians would know this TVO series.

Switchback

Various regions had their own version of this Sunday morning part–game show, part–variety show staple.

Wonderstruck

Bob McDonald broke down everyday science in terms young geeks could understand.

Cancom

Canada has an impressive list of comedy exports, from Michael J. Fox to Jim Carrey to Mike Myers. Here, though, is our list of comic Canucks who made headway and got traction right here at home. Which is no easy feat. *TnT* proudly presents the Short List (named after Martin Short, even though he had to leave Canada to make it really big).

Rick Mercer

Rick has been on TV in this country for twenty-five years straight. To accomplish that is one thing, but to do it at the calibre that Rick does, week after week, is simply unprecedented. As if his dozens of awards and accolades weren't enough, maybe the most telling tale of Rick's #Canadianity is that he's the first to reach the million-point plateau of Air Canada's Aeroplan, with all of his miles travelled in Canada. The prime-time minister of Canada.

Letterkenny Problems

Not unlike *Trailer Park Boys* in that it's a mockumentary snapshot of small-town life, but it's entirely unique in its patois and pacing. Jared Keeso, the co-founder and co-writer, plays lead character Wayne with astonishing restraint, yet somehow brings depth to a classic man-of-few-words country kid. The other *Letterkenny* performances are steady, reserved and nuanced too. But the writing is what sets *Letterkenny* apart. The JPM (jokes per minute) rating is incredibly high, and the true mark of a funny show is that it's found a huge audience by word of mouth. I predict *Letterkenny* will travel as far and last as long as *Trailer Park Boys* for one of the same key reasons: anywhere you go, people know these guys in their own towns.

Picnicface

In the late oughts, a sketch troupe called Picnicface emerged from Halifax. It was eight members big: Andrew Bush, Mark Little, Evany Rosen, Kyle Dooley, Brian MacQuarrie, Cheryl Hann, Bill Wood and Scott Vrooman. Each of them is an incredibly solid performer in their own right, and every one knows their way around a joke.

The main reason they're on this particular list is because they were the first troupe I knew of to blow up on the internet. Their Gatorade parody "Powerthirst" has more than thirty million views and catapulted Picnicface into a new world of cyber-celebrity, earning them comparisons to the Kids in the Hall right out of the gate.

Their TV show on the Comedy Network was funny too, as well as ambitious. I actually did a day on *Roller Town*, their pitch-perfect genre parody feature film.

Codco

Somewhere between *This Hour Has Seven Days* and *This Hour Has 22 Minutes* came *Codco*, the cheeky weekly saucefest from a group of genius Newfoundlanders. In fairness, I'm biased towards this group because they shot in Studio 1 at CBC Halifax, where we shot *Street Cents*, but their absurd observational comedy and outrageous performances made *Codco* must-see CBC programming. Andy Jones, Cathy Jones, Mary Walsh, Greg Malone and Tommy Sexton rewrote the book of what was acceptable by pushing the boundary every single week. I remember as a teenage boy being rapt by the bizarre characters, especially the ones Andy would play. "She had url . . . url on her breastses."

Gerry Dee

When *Mr. D* started, Gerry said, "There are 750,000 teachers in Canada. If they watch, we'll be a hit. Let's make the show for them." From the moment the show started, he's kept that promise, and he analyzes every joke and scenario through the lens of a teacher, watching to ensure that it's plausible.

I've learned a lot from Gerry Dee in the years we've been doing *Mr. D*. Like Jeremy, Gerry isn't afraid to take the time to pursue a joke and make sure it's working. He also deserves kudos for coming into the comedy game relatively late, having worked as a teacher for years first. No one can argue his meteoric rise in the world of standup, and he probably is the undisputed standup-to-sitcom record holder in Canadian TV history.

Russell Peters

We had to include Russell on this list even though, technically, he's made it even bigger everywhere around the entire world than Canada. Not only is he a funny standup, but his true gift is that his comedy reflects an audience that, until he came along, didn't have a voice. He can dissect and distinguish between South Asian countries in a way that leaves audiences rolling in the aisles at his hyper-accurate dialects. Canada has never seen a standup achieve the global heights he has. Nice dude too.

Corner Gas

Brent Butt managed to do something that no one in Canadian TV history had—made a hit Canadian sitcom. There's quite a lesson in how he did it as well. *Corner Gas* didn't try to match the flash of its American counterparts. There was no laugh track, no selling of the material. Just solid jokes, gamely delivered by a competent cast. Sounds easy when you say it like that, but Brent—already one of Canada's foremost standup comics—cracked the TV nut in a way that no one else had. Props to the rest of the cast, led by the masterful Gabrielle Miller and including Canadian treasures Eric Peterson and Janet Wright, plus Fred Ewanuick, Tara Spencer-Nairn, Lorne Cardinal and Nancy Robertson. Deep bench on that show. And now an animated series!

Ron James

Here's another guy who's managed to make a career out of a comedy combo. From *Blackfly* to the long-running *Ron James Show* on the CBC, from coast to coast, from year to year, from town to town, Ron's big vocabulary, staccato delivery and unique take on the Canadian experience keeps them rolling in the aisles and watching on New Year's Eve.

Air Farce

The first troupe that we're aware of to make the successful leap from radio to TV, where their weekly CBC show was watched and adored by millions of viewers every week. Roger Abbott, Don Ferguson, Luba Goy, John Morgan and Dave Broadfoot blew the roof off the Broadcast Centre in Toronto every week at their live tapings. The Tim Hortons set and the Chicken Cannon were always the big draws at the CBC Open House every year. Their undeniable legacy aside, one of the reasons they epitomize BAHDdism is because the Air Farce was notoriously generous and loyal to its crew. Best gig in the business, by all accounts.

22 Minutes

Upon its premiere on TV in 1992, *This Hour Has 22 Minutes* was an instant hit. As in, Greg Thomey and Rick Mercer were catapulted into the stratosphere of fame. Canadian fame, but still. Cathy Jones and Mary Walsh were already famous-ish from *Codco*, but this show sealed the deal. The series has weathered some storms—mostly with casting and recasting issues, particularly in the wake of Rick's departure—and like the town bike of Canadian TV, almost every comedic performer in the country has taken a ride at some point. It's in great hands these days with Mark Critch, Shaun Majumder and unbelievable character performer Susan Kent.

Stuart McLean

A voice like honey dipped in tea, wrapped in bacon and swaddled in cotton nostalgia whose folksy, aw-shucks stories have entertained countless Canucks in books, on the radio and in live shows in every corner of the country. It's scientifically proven that if you listen to a *Vinyl Cafe* story about Dave and Morley, there will be tears. There's a good chance they'll be from laughter.

Canadianity Talk Shows

Many have tried, but few have succeeded, for myriad reasons. Some tried to ape their American counterparts, while others relied too heavily on A-list guests who we just don't have access to "up here." Still others had to rely on Canadian "stars" of upcoming movies of the week, and no one cared.

I don't envy the plight of the Canadian talk show host, and I'm allowed to say so because I was one.

When we started *Jonovision*, the guests on our first few shows acted the way they thought you were supposed to act and tried to channel the *Springer*-esque antics of their southern counterparts. I'll never forget seeing the first promo when it ran on TV. It featured two sisters arguing and one of them said, "Don't even go there, Angela."

Jesus. For the first year, people would say, "You're on that 'Don't even go there, Angela' show, right?"

Mike Bullard

Like him or not, there's no denying Mike managed to do something that had never been done before with a Canadian talk show: make hundreds of episodes. He was always very kind to me and generous with his time when I appeared on *Open Mike*. I also worked with his hilarious brother Pat Bullard on a pilot in the early 2000s. Pat's resumé includes hosting *Love Connection* and being the show-runner on *Reba*. Talented family.

The Hour, with George Stroumboulopoulos

No one can dispute that George has charm, cred and mad interview skills. His casual style puts even the biggest names at ease, often eliciting a "How did you find that clip?" from your Tom Cruises and such. It had a familiar brand with the red chairs, it had an engaging host, it had a solid run at 7 and 11 p.m. I actually worked on George's CNN show, and it was a huge pleasure to watch him work the camera with no teleprompter and nail intro after intro, take after take. One of the best broadcasters Canada has ever seen, full stop.

Dini Petty

The poor (Canadian) woman's Oprah.

Shirley Solomon

The poor woman's Dini Petty.

Camilla Scott

This was the closest we had to Ricki Lake. Camilla was best known as a stage actress—and a darn good one—when CTV gave her a show in an attempt to carve into the booming afternoon talk show universe. Again, Camilla was fine, the topics were on point . . . it just felt like the guests were trying on their shocking revelations like ill-fitting Halloween costumes.

Vicki Gabereau

Vicki is one of the greatest interviewers this country has ever known, and her show was a perfect example of that. If you were interested in the guest, you'd surely dig the chat.

Friday Night! with Ralph Benmergui

I often refer to the "Ralph Benmergui Principle" in Canadian show-biz. When Ralph was co-hosting *Midday* with Valerie Pringle, that show rocked. They had chemistry, she was smart and charming, he was funny. *So* funny. In an environment where you wouldn't expect someone to be. That's the Benmergui Principle.

It's the same reason that "Please welcome a very funny person . . ." is the worst introduction you could ever be given. If I'm sitting in that audience, the first thing I do is cross my arms and think, "With an intro like that, this had better be *awesome*."

All this to say, when the CBC gave Ralph his own glitzy, glossy talk show, *Friday Night! with Ralph Benmergui*, suddenly the stakes were much higher.

Again, let me stress how much respect I have for him. Our paths crossed quite a bit at the CBC and he was always super-kind, helpful and *funny*. So funny. I love Ralph. And he was the obvious and perfect choice to host a late-night show in Canada at that time.

In that environment, though, it didn't work. Ralph is the least of the reasons why. The floor was too shiny, the bits too forced, the guest pool too shallow. Maybe it was simply too American.

Week 1 had Don Cherry and Scott Thompson as guests. Not bad. Then Leonard Cohen. Solid get.

But soon it was the same old Canadian talk show story. The guests were a veritable "Who's that?" of Canadian showbiz.

In season 2, Ralph had a new leather jacket and a new attitude, but by then *Friday Night!* was in the critics' crosshairs and it was too late. Too bad, and not really fair, but *Friday Night!* didn't stand much of a chance to rebound, nor was it given one.

Like the cool cat he is, Ralph landed on his feet and had a great career as a radio broadcaster. Then he moved to Hamilton, so he won at life.

90 Minutes Live

Now, I'm biased on this one because I'm such a Gzowski fan, but I loved this show. Go on YouTube and find Peter's interview with Iggy Pop, or the "Pierre Berton vs. the Cuisinart" segment. Granted, Peter wasn't the most telegenic host ever, and yes, there may have been cigarette ashes on his sweater and ties, but no one can argue it wasn't authentic.

Funny how, at the time, it was determined that Peter was just too uncomfortable to be on TV. In reality, he just didn't fit the mould of a typical host.

The Brent Butt Show

It wasn't a TV talk show, it was a weekly live talk show staged at a club in Vancouver. I happened to be in town one night and took a cab over to see it. As I opened the taxi door, I thought it had started to thunder. Nope. Just Brent absolutely destroying the crowd in his folksy, low-key way. It was the loudest laughter I've ever heard in my entire life. Inspiring.

Award Shows

America has the EGOT, which is the term for someone who wins an Emmy, a Grammy, an Oscar *and* a Tony award. Here in Canada, we have the JuCaGi, and no one to my knowledge has ever won all three—or said that word aloud.

The *Ju* is for Juno, for achievement in music. Taggart has won thousands of Junos with Our Lady Peace. The *Ca* is for Canadian Screen Award, for achievement in television and film. I've won one and lost several. Until 2012, there were two separate categories for film and TV—the Genie Awards and the Gemini Awards. This required the production of two expensive shows, so the Academy (no, not that one) decided to merge the chocolate and the peanut butter. It's now three nights long, to accommodate all the backslapping and deserved recognition. Just to be extra confusing, Quebec has its own Prix Gémeaux, which rewards excellence for artists inside Quebec. As Quebec should.

The *Gi* is for Giller Prize, the top prize for achievement in literature. It's named after the late journalist Doris Giller and was created in 1994 by her husband, Jack Rabinovitch, as a way to honour her. It comes with a lucrative cash award, which might also be why it's now the Scotiabank Giller Prize.

Best Bahds

Think of this as our *TnT* Hall of Canadianity.

The Tragically Hip

Torrens

Much has been written by better and more knowledgeable wordsmiths than I about the cultural significance of the Tragically Hip. The Kingston band somehow managed to bridge the great divide between rural and urban, beer and wine, Queen Street and Main Street.

They also chose to embrace their heritage and celebrate the moments that are distinctly ours. David Milgaard's wrongful conviction in "Wheat Kings." Bill Barilko's disappearance in "Fifty Mission Cap." Referencing the Christie Pits riot of '33 in "Bobcaygeon."

Their reputation as total gentlemen, all class, is widely known too. It's hard to overstate their impact on the musical landscape of this country, on young bands, on young minds.

We tend to judge success based on the amount of traction artists are able to get elsewhere—primarily in the US—but unlike most Canadian artists, the Hip is all ours. They didn't have to leave in order to make a living here.

They didn't have to rely on variety shows or press tours either. Whenever and wherever they played, people showed up. Right until the end, when their two-and-a-half-hour final concert aired on the CBC, consumed by 11.7 million people. The Hip could never be replaced.

John Candy

Taggart

 I know, everyone loves J.C. He's like a band that never gets a bad review, like Radiohead or Ron Sexsmith. People smile when they hear his name. I think it's by design, to be honest. He always said that all he ever wanted in life was to have people like him. I've always asked notable folk if they've ever met him, and if they have, they always respond similarly—"He was the best!" or "The ultimate bahd!" Never have I heard anything bad. It's kind of nuts, because I've asked everyone from former Oilers players to journalists who covered him in Edmonton in the '80s.

My favourite J.C. tale involves the time the Tubes were on *SCTV*. They were guests on *The Fishin' Musician*, a parody of *The Red Fisher Show*, a classic show that ran on CTV from 1968 to 1989 that was soaked in Canadianity. Red would have a guest at his lodge and they would fish all day, then eat what they caught after, all the while having a beauty of a chat.

Apparently, when the Tubes arrived in Edmonton for the taping, a limo picked them up at the airport. The car was stocked to the max with party favourites, and right in the middle of it all was John, just laughing and waving the boys into it. They drank all the way to this lodge that was hours away from Edmonton, and then shot ridiculous footage of fishing and fooling around and a performance, did more partying, and finally made the long drive back to Edmonton. Well, when they got back to the hotel, it was around midnight and they were all banged up. John said to them, "Boys, it's not last call for a couple of hours. Let's hit the clubs!" At this point the Tubes were only able to hit their pillows to crash. John then hit them with "Suit yourself," and the limo went downtown with a solo John.

The life of the party and then some. I think Johnny LaRue was not too far away from John himself—maybe he was LaRue with a huge heart. He just wanted to hang out and enjoy life in the fullest way possible. Clearly it caught up to him, the harshness of that lifestyle, but without the anger and painful, egocentric nature of the typical party person.

Whenever I visit Edmonton, he always pops into my head. It's fun to just cruise around and pretend it's 1983, hoping he might see me and fire a wave. Whenever I meet someone for the first time, I try to make a nice impression. Make them feel like we're in this thing together, and its best we try to enjoy it, because who knows how long we're going to be here.

If there is a heaven, John Candy has a big role in the pearly gates walk-through. Talk about the host with the most! Be sincere. Be more like John Candy.

Mr. Dressup

Torrens

People often ask me who my all-time favourite *Jonovision* guest was. Tough one, because there were so many interesting people on the show over the years. For me personally, broadcasting greats like Ron MacLean, Peter Mansbridge, Scott Russell. It was always fun to have the MuchMusic VJs on the show because they resonated with our audience. Sarah Polley was inspiring.

It's fun to look back and see who appeared on the show and went on to achieve great things. Tegan and Sara. Sum 41. Ryan Gosling.

It should come as no surprise that Tom Green was the craziest guest we ever had. He rolled around in a kiddie pool full of honey and popcorn with a lucky audience member.

It was quite a thrill to have Maestro Fresh Wes on to perform "Let Your Backbone Slide." In recent years, of course, we've worked together on *Mr. D* and I've gotten to know Wes. He's one of the most positive dudes I've ever met and still one of the greatest rap MCs this country has ever known. Certainly the first.

But there was one undeniable favourite. With me, our audience and our crew.

Ernie Coombs. You probably know him better as Mr. Dressup.

He might've been born in the US, but every Canadian between the ages of twenty and seventy-eight will tell you that Mr. Dressup put the "fun" in fundamentals during their childhood development.

The show wasn't fancy or loud, but Mr. Dressup, with the help of his felt posse (Casey, Finnegan, Aunt Bird and Alligator Al), made crafts, sang songs and kept us company.

Never before have I seen someone melt an audience faster than Ernie when he appeared on our show. Teenagers can often be too cool for school or sarcastic, but they instantly softened at the very sight of him.

Over the years, through CBC Kids functions, Ernie and I got to spend some time with together on the road. Walking through an airport with that guy, you'd see people of all ages and stages part like the Red Sea and stare, mouths agape at their childhood idol.

Through it all, Ernie remained humble, warm and befuddled at what all the fuss was about.

One of my prized possessions is a coffee mug that Ernie gave to each of his crew during the final season. It says, simply, TICKLE TRUNK FOREVER.

Jay and Dan Taggart

Jay Onrait and Dan O'Toole are true bahds. I met Jay after a couple of back-and-forth gags on Twitter. I'm pretty sure he was talking about his liking for Popeyes chicken (Dan's favourite!) in a tweet. I replied with my assumption that it's a convenient way to eat, because you can shit through a straw after you eat it. Fast friends. A poop joke is the best way into J & D's hearts.

I began chatting with Jay, and we decided to meet up at Caplansky's Deli in Toronto, right atop Jay's old hood of Kensington Market. Jay turned me on to the insanely tasty pea soup there. Solid as a rock! We had a great lunch chatting about our mutual love of Canadianity, including Al Waxman and Jay's attempt at becoming the next King of Kensington (he was writing a new version of the classic show starring himself), as well as great music. We hit the record/bookstore She Said Boom!, talked music and movies, and we've been great bahds ever since.

Jay invited me on the *Jay & Dan* pod shortly after that, and although I was pretty nervous, it was a great time and I was well received by the fans of the show. So well that I ended up doing a regular segment on the show—reading Jay's travel letters with my incredibly awful Australian accent, telling stories about my dad and tales from the road. I found both Jay and Dan had very similar views to my own, just like bahds do.

The story that probably hooked Jay and Dan was, of course, about human waste . . . and the time my dad got banged up at Christmas dinner.

I made the mistake of getting Dad a bottle of Scotch for Christmas. He started getting belligerent, and my mom had to take him home. There was a bad snowstorm going on and the roads were shitty. Dad had to pee and was asking, in a banged-up manner, for my mom to "Pull the fuck over!" so he could piss. Mom was worried that they'd get stuck in the snow if she got onto the shoulder. He kept ranting and raving until he said, "Okay then, fuck it!" Followed by a pregnant pause . . . then "*Aaaaaahhhh!* I love it!"

Yes, he pissed his seat. With a sick, pleasured face and acceptance. Pretty greasy. Mom wasn't pleased, of course. Dad awoke the next morning with no memory of the events and was sick for three days. He was very sorry for the scene and called us all with apologies. He hasn't touched Scotch since.

That tale went over pretty well with Jay and Dan fans. It was the start of many more classic Ronnie stories.

I went golfing with Dan at Wooden Sticks, a haunt for TSN personalities, because of the horny rate they're given. We laughed the whole round and went to Dan's place for dinner, and of course Dan ordered in Popeyes chicken. I gotta say, it was pretty tasty, and I didn't shit through a straw afterwards!

I'm so thankful to Jay and Dan for giving me the platform to opine upon my life. It's opened so many doors for me since. They got me in with great people at TSN 1050, and Jay hooked me up with the legendary lawyer Gord Kirke, who has helped me with many issues, personal and professional. Jay's also the reason this book is happening with HarperCollins. I met now-former HC editor Doug Richmond out with Jay at a Kensington bar and we started chatting music and books, and here we are!

When Jay and Dan got snapped up by Fox Sports 1 in LA, I was sad, but not surprised. They are very talented, but also very real. Lots of people in media seem like they are super-nice and genuine, but most of the time it's all put on to pander to the public. J & D are the absolute example of legit. Like I said, true bahds! They cemented their cult Canadianity status when they returned home to TSN after Fox Sports 1 cancelled their show in early 2017.

Gordon Lightfoot

Torrens

 My fascination with Gordon Lightfoot started in 2001, when I was working as a writer for the Juno Awards. Bruce Cockburn was being inducted into the Canadian Music Hall of Fame, and it was decided that Lightfoot and David Suzuki would do the honours. It made sense. Suzuki would speak to Bruce's accomplishments as an activist and Gordon would speak to his significant musical accomplishments. (As an aside, I remember when an interviewer asked Eddie Van Halen what it was like to be the best guitar player in the world and he said, "I don't know, ask Bruce Cockburn!")

As part of my research, I started watching old Juno broadcasts. I was certainly aware of Lightfoot and knew the big songs, like "If You Could Read My Mind," "Sundown" and "Rainy Day People," but once I climbed into the wormhole, I was all in. Imagine having access to the entire CBC archives to immerse yourself in on a project like that!

For example, did you know he started out on a CBC show in the '60s called *Singalong Jubilee*? Did you know he was commissioned by the CBC to write "Canadian Railroad Trilogy"? Did you know that sometimes, late at night, as I played his songs on my Martin guitar (because that's what he used), I started to believe I was him?

Okay, that's a bit of a stretch, but "If You Could Read My Mind," you would know that I definitely thought I could potentially play him in a movie of the week.

At least until Taggart laughed so hard at the notion that I couldn't help but laugh too. Oh well. My spotty but spirited Lightfoot impression has found a perfect home on the podcast, co-starring Jeremy Taggart as his manager Bernie.

Terry Fox

Taggart

People like to use the word "great," but sometimes it gets thrown around too much, watered down in its importance. But when it comes to Terry Fox, he redefined the word. Beat it through the mud and reworked it to a diamond finish, clear and deep. *Great*. I was freshly five when Terry dipped his artificial leg into the Atlantic Ocean on April 12, 1980, in St. John's, Newfoundland, to begin his Marathon of Hope.

He ran in the cold, drumming up support as he went, and soon people started to pay serious attention to this phenomenal young cancer patient trying to run across Canada on one leg. Averaging forty-two kilometres a day in awful weather, his foot became blistered and raw. Then there was his artificial leg, made from fibreglass and steel and never designed for running. It bruised and cut its way into the resting stump, slowly digging its way in, day after day.

Imagine the strength and will of this young man. Pressing on in the early days even though nobody came out to support him as he ran through small towns and cities. Just grinding it out through that pain and frustration. Thank God he had acquired the ear of the nation by the time he was making his way through New Brunswick. He was a Canadian hero by the time he got to Ontario, and even though I was only five, I was aware of him by then. I remember him meeting his idol, Darryl Sittler, and receiving his 1980 NHL All-Star Game sweater. The iconic images of Terry running before a throng of people or in the rain alone, trailed by a police car that lit his dreary way in the early morning.

The determination in his eyes also blows my mind. How many people on Earth have faced that goal, with that pain, not to mention the way the cards were stacked against him, yet he pushed on and on. Even when death was the only way he was going to stop running on that highway, he kept hold of that goal.

His words in that final press conference before his death: "That's the thing about cancer. I'm not the only one, it happens all the time to people. I'm not special. This just intensifies what I did. It gives it more meaning. It'll inspire more people . . . I just wish people would realize that anything's possible if you try. When I started this run, I said that if we all gave a dollar, we'd have twenty-two million for cancer research, and I don't care, man, there's no reason that isn't possible. No reason."

I'm proud of a lot of Canadians, but my heart beams a little brighter when it comes to Terry Fox and what he accomplished as a human being. The Bahd of all Bahds.

Game On!

Having some new bahds over and looking for ways to break the ice? Try one of our *TnT* party games! They're not too hard—most have a true-or-false element, which gives you a fifty-fifty shot at getting the answer right—and they teach us about Canadian history. The best part: minimal prep is required.

Canadian or Ca-not-ian

Take turns listing inventions, letting the others guess whether each was invented by a Canadian. Thanks to the Heritage Minute, we all know that James Naismith invented basketball, but how about some trickier ones—the zipper? peanut butter?

Poem Sayin'

Pick famous Canadian songs and challenge each other to read the lyrics aloud with passion but without laughing. To make it harder, give each other characters to play: For instance, read "Don't Forget Me (When I'm Gone)" by Glass Tiger as a New York beat poet in the '60s. Or read "Wave Babies" by Honeymoon Suite as your pervy uncle.

On the Darts

One of our more obscure but oddly addictive games. Wait—is it addictive or addicting?

Either way, pick a group of people. The cast of *Street Legal*. The 1987 Montreal Expos. The rock band Triumph. Go through them one member at a time and speculate as to who's "on the darts" (smokes cigarettes).

Fun, right?

"On the Darts" also works with categories, like Canadian female singers:

- **Alanis**—not on the darts
- **Avril**—darts
- **Anne Murray**—not on the darts anymore
- **Céline**—no darts
- **Shania**—sneaky darts
- **Joni**—Dart City

Hit the Post

Cue up some classic songs on YouTube that have a long TTV (time to vocal). Your job is to vamp over the instrumental part, the way a DJ would, bailing just before the singer starts singing. The longer the intro, the harder this is.

To add a degree of difficulty, you can also give each other a DJ name (Spider Clemons), a day part (weekend mornings) and call letters/mascot of a fictitious station (101.9 The Owl in Carcross, Yukon).

It's surprisingly difficult and unbelievably fun.

Gagnes or Gagnon

Variations on this one include "Shania Twain or Shania Twin."

Take turns playing clips of "famous people" speaking. The contestant has to guess if it's the actual person or André-Philippe Gagnon doing his impression of them. Would work with Rich Little too.

I wonder if there's an André-Philippe Gagnon impersonator out there somewhere? That would be so meta!

Is That Stephen Hawking Talking?

One person pulls clips of Hawking interviews and also records sentences using the app that makes your voice sound computerized. You have to guess whether it's Hawking talking. Fortunately for Jonathan, Jeremy usually wedges a swear word into his sentences, so it's fairly easy to distinguish.

The Holiday Hum-Off

Give each other holiday season scenarios and carols to hum. It's so dumb, but it cracks us up.

For example: "You just found the perfect gift for your wife and you're smugly and calmly walking through the mall completely at peace but surrounded by chaos. Your song is 'God Rest Ye Merry Gentlemen.'"

A big part of making these games fun is knowing that not every name, every improv, every performance will be funny, so just surrender to the silliness.

TnT Is Sketchy

We sort of stumbled upon our improv sketches through playing Top Five jams for different scenarios. "Top Five Opening the Cottage Jams" yielded two women characters from Yellowknife who lived on an island and wore down vests. "Top Five F*ck It, I Quit Jams" bore scenarios where one of us would quit a job in a ball of fury, while the other was the manager. Some are one-offs, like the frigid sexless couple in their sixties, one of whom is proposing a threesome but the other is definitely not into it.

Others stuck, either because they made us laugh or because bahds demanded we bring them back. Here are just a few of the larger-than-life duos in the *Taggart & Torrens* universe.

Salvador and Bre-Ashley

The slimy Sexican perv and the vulnerable doe in the headlights make an unlikely couple, but their passion is undeniable. They met working at White Spot, where she was a server and he was a busboy. She was rattled by his handsy kitchen encounters, but he played the cultural card, explaining he "just don't understand jor

Canadian waysss." His T-shirt puts the "tight" in "You Canadians are so uptight."

Gord and Bernie

A bored Gordon Lightfoot visits his busy manager, Bernie Finkelstein, often arriving through the window to deliver a pan of Nanaimo bars. They're Bernie's weakness. Gord gets irrationally irritated when Bernie is working on business for his other big client, Bruce Cockburn. Our take on this relationship has nothing to do with truth—much like the Vannellis—but the *Odd Couple* dynamic is a proven comedy staple and it makes both of us laugh really hard.

Jer Bear and Colleen in the Morning

Our take on the gender politics of a workplace, set in the confines of a terribly dated FM morning-radio show. Jer Bear makes four times what Colleen does, and their thinly veiled venom for each other is audible to the listeners. Colleen is passive-aggressive, Jer is aggressive-aggressive.

Andrea N Them

Our *TnT* sitcom! From the moment the theme song kicks in ("Only Wanna Be with You" by Hootie and the Blowfish), *Andrea N Them* is every awful sitcom idea in one "show." The laugh track is way too loud. Catchphrases are forced. Plots resolve way too simply. The "Are they or aren't they" is more of a "Who cares if they ever do?"

But the best part of *Andrea N Them* is the very real, relatable friendship between roommates Andrea and Laramie. Andrea is a fun-loving Cape Breton gal who moved up to Toronto (Mississauga) to work at "Purolatorrs." She found Laramie, who was looking for a roommate on "Kijijisss," and they've been inseparable ever since. Their relationship is mostly platonic, although after a few Coronas on the weekend, Andrea might get Laramie to "pretend he's her boyfriend" so some guy will stop ogling her. She's also constantly trying to bait the hook, saying things like "My arse doesn't look very good in these yoga pants—or does it, Laramie?"

Clearly, she would be open to the idea of them pursuing something beyond their roommate relationship, but he's either too oblivious or self-absorbed to notice. For his part, Laramie gets a kick out of Andrea, and she probably gets him out of the house to "shake the stink offa him" more than he's ever been. She isn't on the darts but has been known to succumb to weekend bumsies outside Sneaky Dee's, where she loves the "nat-chose."

The most fun is when there are crossover appearances, like when the Vannelli brothers show up to take Andrea to the Ex. Or Salvador and Laramie butt heads.

Or we introduce a third character and one of us has to play them.

As in *Andrea N Them*, Jeremy is in charge of the theme, the audience laugh track, the audience "ooohs," and playing Laramie *and* Gary Lake, the greasy landlord. My stomach gets right friggy just imagining how much of a mind-melter that is. He's one talented pecker!

That's All He Wrote

When it was getting late into the evening, a friend's dad always said, "Well, Florence, we should get to bed and let these good people get home." That's kind of how we feel about overstaying our welcome on paper. Even though you can pick up or put down this book whenever you like, even though you could have chosen not to read it or stopped at any point, we still want to make sure you had a good time. Canadians, eh? We should care less about what others think and care more about what we think of ourselves.

In any case, we're torqued you made it this far.

If you're not Canadian, hopefully you now feel equipped to handle any poutine party you're ever invited to. That was a test. There's no such thing. Did you pass?

If you are Canadian, hopefully these few hundred pages have reminded you how lucky we are to live here in the way that doing the podcast has reminded us. Hopefully you see being Canadian as a privilege and a responsibility.

So the next time you're travelling to another country with a maple leaf sewn on your backpack, or come across someone on the streets of Montreal without a coat, or witness a frazzled parent struggling to get a stroller into West Edmonton Mall . . .

Hop in. Help out. Smile. Lend a hand. Share a laugh.

That, bahds, is Canadianity.

Special Thanks

Taggart

This book wouldn't exist if it weren't for all the people mentioned in it. I'd like to thank my incredible and beautiful wife, Lisa, and my three kids, John, Jack and Aneliese, for putting up and pushing me to write and finally finish this book. Thank you to my amazing parents, Ronnie and Beryl. Thanks to Jenni, James and Jetsun for being so interesting, I couldn't ask for better siblings or parents, I love you guys!

Thanks to Jonathan Torrens for helping me shape *TnT* into the most enjoyable work environment I've ever experienced, and for cracking the whip to finish this book, and for being such a bahd to me and everyone else! Thanks to Tim Oxford, for being such a great soul, getting our pods out through thick and thin, and for making me so proud with your success! Thanks to Mike MacFarlane for being a ground-floor bahd and for all his work with TaggartnTorrens.ca.

Thank you to all the bahds who listen to us and find common ground with us—it really is everything. Thanks for choosing us to be the soundtrack to long drives, lawn care, baling hay, skating on the pond, sitting by a crackling fire by a lake or working a night shift at the gas station. Thank you, all!

Torrens

Who could ever have guessed when Taggs and I decided to start recording what were essentially weekly phone conversations for our new podcast that a fancy HarperCollins book would be the outcome? Certainly not Jeremy. *I* knew it all along. That's how people tell us apart. I'm the "optimistic" one. He's the one with the "carefree attitude and crazy rock 'n' roll misadventures." Doesn't he sound so much more interesting than me? It's okay. He really is. We're like *The Bahd Couple*.

There are two things that get me all fired up about the relative success of *TnT*. The first is that our instinct was right. That this gorgeous country is crawling with all kinds of bahds like us, who just want to reminisce about their childhoods, have a drink or two and not let things get too heavy. Who see the bright side and try to laugh at the hardships, 'cuz we recognize it's the tough times that make us appreciate the great ones. That #Canadianity is more than just a silly made-up word. It's a meaningful movement.

Second, *TnT* is maybe the most authentic thing I've ever done in my career. It's me being me, warts and all, for better or for high-pitched cackle-y worse. The best part is this: we started doing it for *fun*. It certainly wasn't for the money. So it's not lost on me that the outcome is so satisfying. It's a great reminder that when you choose to do things for the right reasons, the universe takes care of the rest. So, bahds, if there's something (or someone!) you know in your heart you're supposed to be doing, go for it. You'll be amazed at what comes your way. Yes, I know that sounds clich-eh, but trust me, I'm a bahd-liever.

For example, I moved home from chasing "it" in LA because I realized that no job could replace living where I'm from. Canada. I remember the very day when the things that used to feel suffocating and limiting about my home suddenly became comforting and familiar.

Shortly after I moved back to Nova Scotia, I met the love of my life, Carole, and we went halfers on two small roommates. See? The universe rewarded me for making a choice for the right reasons. So I'd like to dedicate my 50 percent of this book to the woman who occupies 100 percent of my thoughts. Carole is my whole universe. She is even smarter than she is pretty, and funnier than she is smart. That's saying a lot, 'cuz she's a total rocket. I really did "marry up." Thanks to the "ghirlst," Sugar-Daisy and Indigo, for making my heart grow extra chambers. And to the Torrenses and MacLeods in my life. I'm a lucky guy to have so much support.

Three more quick dedications. First, to Doug Richmond for commissioning this book, Jim Gifford for seeing it through and everyone else at HarperCollins for holding our hands through this process. Thanks for seeing in us what we had yet to see in ourselves. Your confidence in *TnT* made this possible.

Next to you bahds for sharing this journey with us and invigorating us with your own Canadianity tales. Your emails, tweets and stops on the street fill our hearts with so much joy. Thanks for listening at work, in the car and around the fire in your beer chairs.

And finally, to Jeremy Taggart. Thanks for the laughs, the stories and that *rat-a-tat-tat* machine-gun, joy-filled laugh that echoes in my head whenever there's a moment of silence. Can't think of anyone else I'd rather hear on the other end of the line.